Walter Malone

Songs of Dusk and Dawn

Walter Malone

Songs of Dusk and Dawn

ISBN/EAN: 9783743303508

Manufactured in Europe, USA, Canada, Australia, Japa

Cover: Foto ©Thomas Meinert / pixelio.de

Manufactured and distributed by brebook publishing software (www.brebook.com)

Walter Malone

Songs of Dusk and Dawn

Songs

of

Dusk and Dawn

BY
WALTER MALONE

BUFFALO
CHARLES WELLS MOULTON
1895

COPYRIGHT, 1895,
BY WALTER MALONE.

*TO MY BROTHER,
JAMES HENRY MALONE,
I INSCRIBE THIS VOLUME.*

PREFACE.

THIS volume contains all verses written by me during the last two years, as well as most of those included in "Narcissus and Other Poems," published in 1892, and a few lines from "The Outcast and Other Poems," which appeared in 1885, and "Claribel and Other Poems," printed in 1882.

The earliest of these books was published by me when I was only sixteen years old and the next when I was nineteen. Of course these youthful efforts were very crude and all their lines bore marks of puerility and immaturity. Although the first two books contained together over six-hundred pages, composing the largest works, I believe, ever issued by a minor, I have reprinted from them only a few hundred lines.

I have been tempted to suppress them entirely, but I feel sure that no one will blame me for the love I bear these first-born children of my boyish fancy, which constrains me to spare their lives. And when the critics come with their merciless sickles, I beg them to deal gently with the few little homely wildflowers which I have saved from amid that waste of weeds.

CONTENTS.

	PAGE
PONCE DE LEON	9
NARCISSUS	30
THE MENDELSSOHN WEDDING MARCH	54
"THE LOVE OF WOMAN."	57
"AS MORNING COMES."	59
BETROTHED	60
A GIFT	61
"TO ONE WHO WILL UNDERSTAND."	62
"I LOVE THY FAULTS."	63
L'AMANTE DU DIABLE	64
THE POTTERS FIELD	70
TEMPTED	75
THE RESURRECTION	78
SEPARATED	81
FORTUNE TELLING	82
"I WONDER WHY."	84
LIFE	85
"I KNOW NOT WHY I LOVE THEE."	86
THE REDBIRD	87
THE CAPTIVE MOCKING-BIRD	93
THE REVELLERS	95
OUT OF THE FOLD	99
"WHEN THOU ART NEAR."	103
"TO ONE WHO SHALL BE NAMELESS."	105
HER SECRET	107
"EVERYTHING NEW UNDER THE SUN."	109
ORPHEUS AND THE SIRENS	110
ETERNAL LOVE	118
"JESUS WEPT."	121

Contents.

THE GRAVEYARD	124
A VANISHED SUMMER	126
THE ONE LOVE	129
"HE WHO HATH LOVED."	130
UNSPOKEN LOVE	131
"THOU LITTLE DREAMEST"	132
SONNET	133
A BRIDAL BALLAD	134
THE BYRON CENTENARY—1788-1888	137
A WEDDING SONG	138
THE FIRST TRANGRESSION	140
GLADSTONE	142
DYNAMITE	144
SHELLEY	147
WILL HUBBARD KERNAN	148
A MODERN JULIET	149
THE PRINCE'S WEDDING	151
ELIZABETH AND ESSEX	157
MY QUEEN	160
WHEN I GET RICH	161
THE POSTMAN	165
BYRON	167
TO DR. J. J. WHEAT	169
A VISION IN ASHES	171
A FIRESIDE PHANTOM	173
TRIUMPHANT LOVE	178
THE OLD COLLEGE DAYS	180
THE MOCKING-BIRD	183
"YE BACHELOR."	190
A FLOWER FROM THE GRAVE OF SHELLEY	193
THE LITTLE WANDERER	195
"SCORN NOT THE HEART."	198
CONFIRMATION	199
"MARY."	200
"BACK TO THE WORLD."	202

Contents.

FRAGMENTS FROM
"THE OUTCAST AND OTHER POEMS."

Morning	205
Evening	205
Autumn	206
Three Southern Scenes	208
To One Departed	212
The Cynic	213
A Storm in Summer	214
"The Beginning of the End."	217
Martyrdom	219
The Poet	219
Before the Battle	219
The Battle	220
The Spring	221
Patriotism	222
March	222
A Father's Curse	223
"The One Thing Needful."	223
In Paradise	224
Stanzas to Madeline	225
Callista	226
On a Lock of Marie Antoinett's Hair	229
Delia	232
Mortality	233
A Wish	234
The Bard	235

FRAGMENTS FROM
"CLARIBEL AND OTHER POEMS."

Inez	239
Realized Hopes	241
Despair	241
The Coming of April	242

Contents.

THE HUMMING-BIRD	246
A WINTER MIDNIGHT	248
OPPORTUNITY	248
THE VICTOR	248
LOVE AFTER DEATH	248
ONE SUMMER	249
TRIBUTE TO SHELLEY	253

SONGS OF DUSK AND DAWN

PONCE DE LEON.

I.

AT midnight Ponce de Leon stood alone
  Beneath the grey sails of his sea-worn ship,
His fierce eyes faded by the flight of years,
His broad brow withered by a thousand toils.
Around him spread the boundless southern seas,
Above him hung the mystic southern skies;
Seas never plowed by ships of men before,
The phantom gateway to a phantom world,
Unfolding marvels in their magic isles
Held close in secret since the world began:
Skies that have never seen their realms revealed
Though watched and gazed upon six-thousand years,
With starry isles that saw the birth of Time,
Whose godlike glories none shall ever know.

The mighty yellow moon began to rise,
Beyond the gaunt palms of a rocky isle
In all the golden glory of the south,
Undimmed through ruins of the myriad years,
Revealing secrets of this new-found world,
Herself a secret never to be told.

And Ponce de Leon lingered still alone,
For none among his sailors knew his plans,

And none could understand his vague, vain dreams;
And though his feet were treading in their midst,
His soul was sailing in a ship alone,
Upon an ocean in another world.
And then he spoke in whispers to himself:
"I see the moon rise as in years of yore
She rose above the Andalusian skies,
And silvered castle turrets on the heights,
And haunted grottos far away in Spain,
A wondrous blossom fading night by night,
And yet renewed in splendor evermore.

"But those who watched her with me when a boy,
Have passed forever from the sight of men,
And left me grey and lone and desolate,
A relic of a generation dead.
A thousand leagues of ocean sweep and swirl
Between me and their graves in distant Spain;
The same old moonlight trembling on their tombs
Far, far away in scenes of perished years,
Across the waves of ocean wild and wide
Now trembles on me, treading earth alone,
Surrounded by the youthful and the gay,
Dissevered from old faces that I knew,
A living spectre of the vanished years.

"In days long perished, with this loyal sword,
I smote the Moors on many a battlefield,
Or fought the savage in this new-found world;
But now it quakes and quivers in my hand,

And now its keen edge cankers into rust.
The younger soldiers see me with a smile,
And whisper that my time has passed away.
Then, all the grand old friends that once I knew,
With whom I braved the perils of the deep,
When bold Columbus sailed the trackless seas,
Have left me, passing to another world
Whose seas forever shall be unexplored.

"Once, in those dear days, ere my raven hair
Was flecked with frost of melancholy years,
When my young heart seemed full of summer
    warmth,
And the fresh fragrance of the flowery fields;
When sunny skies hung in a mellow maze
And all the world was wreathed in garlands green;
When pearly peach blooms in the orchards blew,
And tuneful thrushes wove their happy nests,
I wandered with a maiden whom I loved,
The fairest and the sweetest of the earth.
Ah well I now remember when she said
'I love you,' how the tell-tale robins trilled;
And when I kissed her loving little lips,
The dewy daisies kissed her little feet.

"But then we parted by the dear old gate,
Beside the roadway leading to the town;
And as I clasped her ere I went away,
We vowed to love each other evermore.
But leagues of desert, mountain, wold and wave

Came in between us, as an awful storm
Dissevers two ships far away at sea;
And yet we loved each other all the more,
Longing to press each other's lips again,
To gaze once more within each other's eyes,
To speak once more the old, old words of love.
But year by year sped swiftly, and at last,
We both grew grey beneath their wizard wings.
So when at last we two had met again,
Both shrank back, startled, at the fearful change.

"Ah, poor old woman! All thy golden locks,
Had grizzled long before to grey, while age
Plucked, one by one, the roses from thy face,
And dimmed with winter's tearful twilight gloom
The summer splendor of thy dear blue eyes.
My boyhood bloom had vanished from my face,
And left an old man, poor and desolate.

"Alas! I dare not tell the hateful tale
Of disappointment and of chill despair,
Of how I shunned her and she turned from me;
How all the leagues of ocean and of earth
Had bound us closer with a chain of love,
And yet the years had stolen in between,
And like a throng of traitors, slow but sure,
Had separated us forevermore.

" Since we have parted, I have roamed the world
To find the Fount of Youth, whose crystal waves

Shall make us young again; but evermore
My dreams and visions all are doomed to die.
The crafty red men, wishing to be free
From pillage of my soldiers, ever tell
Of this, the mystic fountain of my dreams,
As being just beyond their native lands.
Yet as I journey onward, hoping still,
They ever point me further to the north;
And so I seek forevermore in vain.
But I shall never cease to journey on,
Until I find Immortal Youth, or Death."

II.

All worn and weary with his weight of cares,
He sank in troubled slumber on the deck.
He dreamed he wandered through a desert waste
Of red sands, parching underneath red suns,
Where withered rocks were never decked with dews,
Nor shriveled skies refreshed with cooling clouds;
But flamed forever with a feverish fire,
Like aching eyes too sore with grief for tears;
Where bubbling fountains, blossoms, birds and trees,
Had not existed since the world began.

His feet were bleeding on the cruel flints,
His tongue was throbbing with a maddening thirst;
At last he sank upon the sands to die:
Then, ere he closed his eyes, far, far away,

Where the red sun was rising in the east
Like a great giant rousing in his wrath,
He saw the snowy peaks and plumy palms
Of an oasis green as emerald.

Then all his hopes revived like fading flowers
That open to the patter of the rain;
He roused himself and journeyed on again,
Until he reached that peerless paradise.
And when his aching limbs reposed at last
On dewy mosses by its silvery springs,
He laughed and shouted with a frenzied joy,
Till reason came again to soothe his soul,
And then he gazed around in wonderment.

Magnolias waved their glossy boughs of green,
With great white blossoms bursting into bloom,
Like moonlight on the bosom of a swan;
The golden jasmines swung their chalices,
And scattered such sweet odors on the air,
That blithesome breezes swooned and reeled with
    joy,
And kissed them dying in delicious love;
The frail wild roses trembled on their stems,
Like modest maidens robed in spotless silk;
The redbird flamed amid the verdant boughs,
A royal ruby in an emerald throne;
The bluebird, like a feathered violet,
Whose fragile fragrance vanished in a song,
Played with the humming-birds, whose jeweled
    wings

Would sparkle like a dazzling shower of gems;
The mock-bird sang with all his fervent soul,
As though the ghost of some great bard of old
Had come to live in bosom of a bird,
With tongue of silver and a heart of gold.
And there, amid the blossom-tangled vines,
The trembling leaflets and the trilling birds,
A crystal fountain, like a storm of snow
Leaped in its sparkling splendor far on high,
In clouds of plumy vapor, frosty spray
And dazzling dew-drops, with their diamond hues.

Beside it, stood a maiden, bright as morn,
A crystal goblet brimming in her hands
With bubbling radiance, like a crown of gems
Or like a spotless, palpitating star.
A gauzy garment fluttered round her limbs,
Too frail to hide her lustrous loveliness;
And there she stood, so pure, diaphanous,
The sunlight through her crystal splendor shone,
And one might see the pearly lily bells
Shine through the wine-like beauty of her breasts,
And feathery ferns through light, transparent arms,
While humming-birds were tangled and ensnared
Amid the mazes of her golden hair,
And frailest water lilies bended not
Beneath the tripping of her rosy feet.

She motioned him, the gray-haired mariner,
To drink the sparkling goblet that she gave

Out of the fountain of undying youth;
But ere his lips could quaff the limpid stream,
He woke to find it vanished from his sight,
To find his anxious comrades gathered round,
Awaked and startled by his dreamful sighs;
To see, with weary eyes, the same old world,
And the old story of its tears and toils.

III.

Resplendent morning, flushed and passionate,
With eyes a-sparkle and with cheeks aflame,
Sinks in the white arms of the panting day;
And like a young bride on her nuptial night,
When first her lover sees her virgin breast,
Averts her eyes beneath his burning gaze,
Then leaps with fervor on his blazing heart,
Consumed within the white heat of his love,
Its swoonful blisses and delirious joys.

Along the sandy coast of Florida
The proud palmettos lift their serried spears,
The giant grapevines twist their snaky arms
In monstrous coils around the live oak limbs;
The verdant creepers cling to rotten trunks,
With crimson-clustered blossoms thrusting forth,
Like bloody fingers of a murderer's hand.
The wondrous wildwoods with their emerald shades
Are like the forests under ocean waves,
Where mellow amber blossoms in jasmine sprays,
Where dogwood blossoms hang like lustrous pearls,

And red buds glimmer like a coral grove;
Where dead trees lie like masts of sunken ships,
And humming-birds flit through the verdant gloom,
Like jeweled fishes flashing golden fins.

The red flamingoes throng the sandy coast,
Like splashes of a bloody sunset sky;
The snow-white pelican, the awkward crane,
Tread with the spoon-bill in the shallow bay;
While far above, a secret evermore,
The ancient sacred ibis floats along.

All day they sail along the yellow coast;
All day they gaze upon the wondrous woods;
All day they watch the red flamingoes flame,
And see the ibis circling through the skies.
But still they see no face of living man,
No cheerful cottage and no curling smoke,
As though the land were Adam's paradise
Where nevermore his banished sons shall tread.

And now the evening, like a Bacchanal,
In all the splendor of her streaming hair,
In all the flush of madness jubilant,
Arrayed in purple and in cloth of gold,
Lifts in the skies her chalice crystalline
And splashes all the clouds with rosy wines,
Tingling and trembling with voluptuous thrills,

Amid her throngs of frenzied revelers,
Till all the spectral shadows of the night,
Like stealthy foemen at some ancient feast,
Creep in with daggers of the flashing stars
And slay them in the blossom of their bliss.

Again the moonrise in the mystic night,
Again the glimmer of the silent stars,
Again the secrets never to be told,
Again the lonely vigil in the gloom!

Once more the grey-haired sailor stands alone,
Beneath the grey sails of his sea-worn ship;
Once more he dreams of scenes in perished years,
Of faces in the tomb of long ago.
He wanders through the fields that once he trod,
In blithesome boyhood, far away in Spain;
He sees the village just beneath the hill,
He sees the vineyards and the cottages,
He sees the peasants toiling in the fields;
The birds are singing as in days of old,
The bees are booming in the clover blooms
Just as they boomed around him when a boy.
He hears the children laughing in the lanes,
And almost thinks he hears them call his name,
And beg him join them in their happy play.
He sees the foolish lovers wooing still
Beneath the peach-blooms, while the mild-eyed dove
Peeps at them as she hovers in her nest.
He sees the old spring with its little brook

In which he waded when a bare-foot boy;
Here stands the old stile where he met her first;
Here lies the lane where first he told his love,
The ancient oak that saw him press her hand,
And saw him steal his first kiss from her lips,—
Then the old gate that saw their fond farewell.

But all the dear young faces that he knew,
Are sleeping yonder on the lonesome hill;
All,—all but one! his heart can not forget
Yon poor old woman tottering up the road,
With slouching bonnet and with wooden shoes,
Bent almost double o'er a knotty stick,
Bearing a basket with a few scant herbs,
Gathered together for her meagre meal.
Too well his heart remembers, long ago,
This poor old crone was young and beautiful,
Though now all grizzled, gaunt and full of pains,
A ruined relic, scorned by all the world,
That only loves the young and gay and fair;
Forgotten by them all save one old man
In this lone world, a thousand leagues away!

He knew that soon for her the end would come,
Thus toiling feebly as the days went by.
"My God, my God!" he faltered through his tears,
"Grant me the power to find the magic fount,
That I may save her, make her young again,
Ere all my toils may be too late, too late!"

IV.

Day after day they sailed along the coast,
Until they reached a river, deep and broad.
Day after day they sailed its green expanse,
Seeking with sorrow for the Fount of Youth.

Day after day comes laughing in the east,
Day after day lies bleeding in the west;
Day after day hope blossoms in their hearts,
Day after day their hopes are doomed to die.

But the great river narrowed in their course,
Or spread its waters into shallow bays,
Until at last they reached a tangled pass,
Where the good ship could sail no further south.
The broad lush lily pads, with myriad blooms,
Like snares of Sirens meshing peerless pearls,
Threw mazy network all around the prow:
The cypress and the live-oak threw their limbs
Like giant arms to bar them on their way;
The grapevines and the creepers joined above
And like a cobweb tangled in the mast;
The scaly alligators on the logs
Were strewn across the islands and the bays
Like hideous dragons of the days of old,
Guarding the gold fruit of Hesperides.

The heron, standing stiffly, looking wise,
With one foot resting in the water cress,
Seemed mocking at him with a lazy leer;

The gay kingfisher, garbed in gaudy robes,
Seemed smiling at him and his foolish quest;
The crane flew o'er him on her spectral wings
Like a white ghost of dead and buried years;
The radiant redbird paused amid his flight,
To see the stranger in this western world.
Lost in the mazes of his deep despair,
The gray-haired sailor heeded none of them,
Save a sweet mock-bird in magnolia boughs,
Whose soft songs soothed his bleeding heart like balm.

Then with a faltering voice he gave command
To turn the vessel northward in return,
Though like a bird hemmed in an iron cage
His soul still beating at its prison bars,
Was raging at its fetters and its chains,
And longing to pursue its visions still.

That night he pondered long unto himself,
Upon the sphinx-like riddle, Life and Death.
"Alas!" he murmured, "ages fade away,
And desolation conquers all at last.
Like mists of morning nations disappear,
Like leaves of autumn kingdoms quiver by.
As Egypt perished with her hoary kings,
As gray Assyria saw her columns fall,
So all our empires, with their myriad souls,
Shall be the same old idle story still;
And countless kingdoms that shall follow them,

Like them shall vanish in the same old tomb.
Age follows age, till earth is shriveled up,
For all the universe is but a grave.
Why live, if youth shall ever end in age?
If death shall ever triumph over life?
What mean our petty triumphs and our toils
If all are offerings at the shrine of death?
Could I but find the blessed fount of youth,
I would be greater than the kings of earth,
Than all immortal poets of the past,
Than all the prophets and the priests of God.
But nevermore my hopes shall come to pass;
So all the world shall perish with my dream."

And then in troubled sleep he treads again
His boyhood pathways, far away in Spain;
Once more he wanders by the mossy brook,
Once more he sees the windmill on the height;
Once more he treads the orchards, all abloom
With crimson clover and with pearly peach;
Once more he sees the village, old and quaint,
Through whose dull streets he trod so long ago,
Before he yearned to roam around the world,
And seek his fortune in the courts and camps;
Once more he sees the house where he was born,
And then, alas! the graveyard on the hill.

But soon he sees, with looks of deep dismay,
A throng of peasants treading up the hill,
Poor, simple creatures, dressed in coarsest garb,

With threadbare doublets and with wooden shoes.
Before them walks an ancient barefoot friar,
With eyes downcast upon a crucifix;
Then four stout yeomen follow close behind,
And bear a box-like coffin, rough and rude,
Wherein he sees a woman's furrowed face;
Her withered hands are folded on her breast,
Her wrinkled eyelids now forever closed.
But no one weeps above her pallid corpse
And no one sighs to see her pass away
Save this old man, far in a western world,
Whose heart is buried in her humble grave.

v.

THE days dragged on, and Ponce de Leon strove,
With patient hands to conquer Florida;
To build a city and to till the fields,
And make a goodly province for his king.

His feet were worn, yet he had found no rest;
His hands were feeble, yet had toiled in vain;
His eyes were dim, yet he had never seen
The mystic marvels of the magic fount.
All hope had vanished from his withered heart,
Yet still he lived, as in a weary dream;
But life, which long had kept awake his woes,
Was soon to bring him to the bitter end,
To tread the hideous border-land of death,
Where dark despair eclipses every star.

One cloudless day, when pensive evening pined
Above the tropic forests of the west,
After a bloody battle bravely won
Against the crafty Indians of the land,—
Won in a manner worthy of the man
Who plucked the crimson flower of his fame
Not on a carpet, but a bloody field,—
He wandered from the outskirts of his camp,
And sat beside the margin of a pool:
A little pool it was, fed by a brook,
That twisted like a serpent through the grass,
Half choked with reeds and rushes and with mint.
The lakelet was so clear that one might see
Its sandy bottom, fathoms five below,
And watch the writhing fishes wave their fins,
With shining scales, and twirling, twisting tails,
And gaping jaws and huge and glassy eyes,
Like grotesque phantoms in a haunted land.
The swallows dipped amid the dewy spray,
The heron stood amid the water weeds
And watched the gray coot diving in the depths,
The blue-jay in a scaly sycamore
Cried as she saw a black snake slide below;
The staid woodpecker crowned with crimson plumes
Climbed slowly up an oak-tree's aged trunk.
The brown thrush fluttered to her cosy nest,
Where, like a rougish gypsy maiden's eyes,
The round blackberries, gemmed with diamond dew,

Seemed peeping at her as she sank to rest.
An oriole, arrayed in royal robes,
Shown with the mingled glory and the gloom
Of orange sunrise and of sable night.

Long sat he there, and dreamed of other days,
Till sombre twilight trod the forest depths,
Draped all the splendor of the sunset skies
And robed the woods in funeral garb of gray.

But with the death of that eventful day,
The gray-haired sailor was to met his doom;
For in the shades a stealthy foeman crept,
Nearer and nearer, with a sharpened spear.

Then all at once the Indian leaped in view,
And pierced him through his armor with the spear;
The old man struck the savage to the ground,
And slew him with his ever-trusty sword.

He called his comrades, in the camp near by,
Who bore him in a litter to the ship,
But sought in vain to cure his mortal wound.

Scarce could he speak; yet gathered strength at
    last,
To bid them turn to Cuba, on the morn;
So they obeyed him, trimmed the ready sails,
To bear him southward, there to see him die.

But ere he left, there came a zealous priest
To breathe the gospel in his deafened ears,
And point its pathway to his fading eyes;
He held the crucifix where one might see
The writhing Christ nailed to the cruel tree.

"O, Ponce de Leon," spake he solemnly,
"Long hast thou searched to find the fount of youth,
But seen thy searches evermore in vain:
And thou hast found that drink where'er thou wilt,
Thy thirst returns and thou must drink again;
Yet, as thou searchest, still thou growest old,
And as thou seekest thou shalt surely die.
But, hapless man, the fountain shall be found,
And I shall show it to thy fading eyes:
For if thou drinkest of the well of Christ,
Thy thirst shall pass away forevermore,
And drinking of that well thy youth returns,
And thou shalt dwell in palmy Paradise,
Forever happy and forever young."

But Ponce de Leon beckoned him away,
And turned his dim eyes from the crucifix.
"Oh, thou hast been deceived," the priest replied,
"But God will keep His promises to thee."

Still Ponce de Leon beckoned him away,
And still refused to see the crucifix.

"Unhappy man," the priest replied again,
"Like mildew on thy hopes and happiness,
Descends the curse of infidelity,
Which holds the scepter in the shades below,
Where demons laugh to see one flee from God.
Come back, come back! It is not yet too late
To reach the portals of thy Father's home,
Where saints and seraphs with their starry crowns,
Bask in the sunlight of the smile of God,
And wait to welcome thee on thy return
With sounds triumphant like the swelling sea.
Look up to Heaven! seest thou no signal there,
No smile of seraph, and no helping hand?
Seest thou no torch to guide thee in the gloom?
Seest thou no golden city, far away?
Behold the Lamb of God, and thou shalt live!
Cry out to Christ, and He shall comfort thee!"

The dying warrior turned his haggard face:
First tried to speak, then feebly shook his head,
As if to say "No! I shall hope no more:
All, all are fables; I will not believe:
For you deceive me as the rest have done."

The priest fled horrified, and left him there,
To die the death of those who turn from God.

The sails were spread, the harbor soon was cleared,
The vessel glided far away at sea.
The old priest watched it, through his blinding
    tears,

Till the gray sails had faded from the skies;
A ship of death, that bore one to his tomb:
A ship of death, doomed by the curse of God!

———o———

Still beams the moon on Andalusian hills,
As in the dead years of the long ago
When Ponce de Leon and the maid he loved
In blissful silence heard each other's hearts
Beating together with a bounding bliss,
And told each other with their eager eyes
The sweet old story that shall ever live
When kings and queens have crumbled in the clay,
And all the empires of the earth are dust.

The moonbeams falter on her grassy grave,
Upon a lone hill, far away in Spain,
While he is sleeping in his sepulchre
Beyond the oceans of the western world.
The foolish lovers, in their thoughtless bliss,
Still woo each other as they tread the fields
Where those two lovers, centuries ago,
First told their passion to each other's eyes.

Still shines the sun in skies of Florida,
With all the glory of the yester-years,
When Ponce de Leon trod her wondrous woods,
To find the fountain of immortal youth.
Another people rules her palmy plains,
Another nation, with another tongue:

Yet never has the mystic marvel of the fount
Arisen before the eyes of mortal man.

Like him, we long to see its crystal waves,
When old age, like November, chills the skies,
And all our dead hopes, like her withered leaves,
Are falling at the coming of the night.
Like him, we long to see our youth again
Bring back the withered roses of the past,
The mirth of May, and joys of jeweled June,
When April buds are all forever dead,
And suns of summer have forever set.
Like him, we see our toils are all in vain:
Like him we see that we are growing gray:
We seek forever, and we never find,
And as we seek it, we shall surely die.

NARCISSUS.

I.

THE morning flamed above the Doric hills
In all the joyous glory of her youth,
As though her roses would be red forever,
And deck the wide earth with unfading bloom.
Her sparkling eyes dimmed all the night's wan stars,
Her red cheeks tinged the clouds with crimson fire,
While silvery arrows from her worlds of light
Dispersed the grim shades from the verdant woods.
The lithe stag started from his grassy couch
And shook the dew-drops from his branching horns,
The falcon spread his light wings to the winds
And darted upward like a sharpened spear;
The herdsman led his oxen to the brook,
Whose wavelets wondered at the great round eyes;
Then merry laughter from the roguish fauns
Resounded keenly through the leafy dells;
But louder than them all, some piping sprite
Made liquid music with the warbling birds.
But soon Narcissus left his flowery couch,
Narcissus, ever young and beautiful!
And there amid resplendent beams of morn,

Amid the odorous blossoms soft and sweet,
And wildly graceful spirits of the woods,
Narcissus shone the wonder of them all.
No red deer's skin, no tawny lion's hide,
No woven fabric round his shoulders hung,
For young Narcissus roamed in beauty nude;
His soft round limbs, fair as a lily's buds,
Were never hidden in a useless garb.

The flush of boyhood still adorned his face,
A childish beauty budding into youth;
He scampered nimbly like a half-grown god,
With shrill songs varying to a deepening bass.
Sweet little dimples flitted round his mouth,
His curving arms were lovely as a babe's,
His little feet like frail and tinted shells,
With tiny peeping toes like purest pearls.
His roguish eyes bent downward timidly,
As though ashamed to see his nakedness;
His golden ringlets hung upon his breast,
Too short to hide his sweet enchanting charms.

The nymphs beheld him in his boyish grace,
Enraptured by his rounded, naked limbs,
Drinking his beauty like some wondrous wine,
That makes the blood burst into flowers of flame,
Their bosoms madly throbbing, eyes afire,
Breath wildly panting in an eager love,
So that they longed to clasp him in their arms
Forever in delirious blissful swoons.

And often all day would they follow him,
Untiring, through the distant woods and fields;
They'd stroll beside him, call him by pet names,
Clasp his soft cheeks and stroke his curly hair.
Oft would they leap upon him from the ferns,
And kiss his sweet lips o'er and o'er again,
Or madly beg him for one word of love,
Or one embrace to give them in return.
The pretty boy, half angered, like a child,
Would pout, then laugh, half relishing their love.

But often, wearied of their close pursuit,
He longed to wander lone and unharassed;
In vain, for everywhere the roguish spies
Would watch his path and haunt his flying feet.
Through meadows, fields, and forests deep and dark,
Still grottoes, lonely dells, high mountain-tops,
By winding rivers, lily-covered lakes,
He sought in vain for peaceful solitude.

Among the nymphs who thus would follow him,
Poor Echo vexed him more than all the rest;
And while his cunning thwarted other eyes,
This maiden always wandered at his side.
Full oft when gathering violets in the dells,
And thinking him unseen, he'd quickly start
To feel a burning kiss upon his lips,
And see her lithe form swiftly vanishing;
Full oft, beneath some hoary oak's green boughs,

His tired head resting on a bank of moss,
While sleep was weaving meshes round his eyes,
Would hear wild words of deep despairing love,
Sad, soulful sighs, with fond reproaches breathed,
And waking, there behold two great dark eyes
Bent o'er him, and a passion-heaving breast
His pillow, that had first been mossy earth.

Again, while wandering through the caverned hills,
Amid the shades would Echo glide along,
Clasp his soft hands within her fingers wan,
The hot tears trickling down her wasted cheeks,
And sob and murmur of his cruelty.

A curse had long been laid on Echo's head
By jealous Here, heartless in her hate.
For Echo often had assisted Zeus
In hiding amorous sins from Here's eye,
Till being seized at last, confessed her guilt,
And felt the fury of the queen of heaven.
Perfidious Zeus refused the nymph to shield;
So she was banished from the god's abode,
To wander lonely through the waste of Earth,
Where rove swift-fated mortals to the grave,
And Autumn blights the glory of the year;
To pine amid the solemn wilderness,
And long for high Olympus, lost forever.

And Echo was not fair or beautiful,
But plainest, darkest of the woodland nymphs;

Her form had faded to a flitting shade,
Her voice had pined into a mournful cry.
Her eyes were large, dark as a cavern's gloom,
Her tresses like the dusky clouds of night;
Her face was like a specter, and her sighs
Like bitter moaning of the winter winds.
Each word that reached her would her tongue repeat,
For so the high gods cursed her for her sins.
She loved the shades, the solemn solitudes,
The lonely grottoes and steep mountain sides;
So while she haunted close Narcissus' path,
She dared not show her visage openly,
But stole behind him ever stealthily,
And vanished when he turned to speak reproach,
Or, when he sat, would hide in thickets near,
And gaze upon him from the sullen shades.

Sometimes Narcissus, out of cruel spite,
Would wound her heart with stinging jealousy
When smiling on some other rival nymph,
Who madly kissed or fondly folded him.
Her dark eyes glittered with a blasting woe
To see him laughing on a swelling breast,
Some nymph with round arms close embracing him
And drinking in his lovely boyish charms.
But oft Narcissus scorned the charms of all,
And on this morning shunned each maiden's face.

II.

The first who met him as he tripped along
Was one who hunted there with Artemis,
A stately maid with waving ebon hair,
With cheeks as crimson as the popy's bloom,
With dark and wondrous splendor-streaming eyes,
And queenly brow of softest olive hue;
She seemed like dusky twilight, gemmed with stars
And sprinkled by the bleeding heart of day.
Her pure white feet with golden sandals decked
Were stainless and as soft as Eros' wings;
Her green cloak waving in the morning wind
Betrayed a rounded bosom like a swan.
Upon her back a bow and quiver hung,
Within her hand a sharp and shining spear.

"Is this Narcissus?" said she, with a smile;
"I've seen thee in these hills but once before;
Yet one so beautiful no eye forgets,
And so my memory can not be at fault.
But hark, my pretty boy, a face like thine
Will often carry with it deep despair:
The nymphs whose love is scorned are plotting now
To have revenge upon thee. This I know.
For on Olympus only yester-eve
I saw a throng of these with Nemesis,
The stern-browed spirit, feared of gods and men,
Whose only joy is marring lives like thine.
I heard them murmur at thy cruelty,
Then beg dark Nemesis to curse thee, boy,·

And she, I think, assented. Watch them well,
For much I fear some evil day will come."

"Was Echo there?   'Tis like her spiteful way;
I always hated her, and always shall."
"Thou wrong'st her, foolish boy; she was not there,
She long ago was driven from on high.
I can not tell thee more, for hark, oh, hark!
The deep-mouthed hounds are baying through the
    woods,
In hot pursuit of some affrighted stag.
Ye gods! My heart leaps in exulting joy,
And all my veins are tingling for the chase:
Farewell, I follow swiftly to the hunt."

"What thanks, fair goddess, shall I offer thee? —
But yet, alas! I have no gift of worth."

"A gift, thou foolish boy?   Give me a kiss;
For kisses from a young man's amorous mouth
Will buy from woman more than gems and gold.
Another kiss! Another! Clasp again!
Just one more kiss, Narcissus, then I go!
My mistress would reproach me for this act,
But for its joy I'd bear her frown forever.
Beware, O youth. Echo thou needst not fear;
She loves thee as the banished god loves heaven,
But would not harm thee to regain her throne."

Narcissus stood stunned with a curdling fear.
The smile died on his quivering, ashen lips,

His heart grew numb, his youthful blood grew cold,
"Why should they wish to harm me?" muttered he;
"Am I not free to turn away from them?
Shall I be blamed because I love them not?
Shall I be blamed because they pine for me?"

Soon turned he on his heels, and musing went
Along the brook, then sat beneath an elm.
He paused a while, then, growing restless, turned
And lay upon his back, while his fair locks
Were pillowed on a bank of feathery ferns.
But then the sun, arising high in heaven,
Sent through the parted boughs a tiny beam
That fell upon his eyes and made him wince,
So that he leaped up, restless and annoyed.
Soon sitting down again, he dipt his feet
Within the crystal waters just below,—
Those beauteous feet, more soft and sweet and white
Than all the spotless water-lilies there.
The wavelets kissed their blue veins delicate,
And fondled them, and babbled petting sounds,
While silvery minnows, growing bold at last,
Began to nibble at the tiny toes,
Which tingled till they blushed like rose-buds pink,
When he, to rout the minnows, shook his foot,
Splashing the water into foaming spray,
And sent them scampering up the brook in fright,
To peep back at him through the water-cress,
And wonder at his roguish, ringing laugh.

He gazed upon his image in the brook,
And marveled at his own enchanting charms;
His cheeks like ruby wines, blue eyes, bright hair,
The rounded, flower-like beauty of his form.
He blushed to see his utter nakedness
And that which mortals seek to hide from sight,
But felt a boyish pride and secret joy
To feel and see his manhood drawing near.
He knew no maiden could resist his beauty,
And in his heart exulted at the thought.
"I'll scorn them all," he said unto himself,
"And drive them mad to get one stingy smile.
I'll rule them, chained before me by thier love,
And they shall long in vain to kiss my feet."

Then turning round, he saw Leona there,
With jealous passion burning in her eyes;
For much she craved the sweetness of his charms,
But hated him because his heart was cold..

"Leona!" faltered he; "art spying still?
I am aweary of thy hateful eyes."
"Narcissus!" cried she, quickly, "I am mad,—
Mad with fierce love and flaming jealousy.
Beware! Beware! lest thou shouldst force my soul
To bring destruction on thy helpless head."

"Leona, I defy thy silly threats.
I am the son of water-god and nymph:

Free I was born, and free will ever be.
I am immortal; what have I to fear?
For Zeus himself can never take my life,
And thou art but a weak and wandering sprite."

"I know, Narcissus, thou couldst never die,
But, selfish creature, I may curse thee still;
I may call down such anguish and despair
That life itself would be an agony.
Be mine, Narcissus! hearken to my prayer!
Be mine, or I will curse thee and myself!"

"Begone! Begone!" he cried, impatiently,
And turned his eyes in anger from her face,
Looking towards the woods beyond the brook.
A deadly silence seemed to shroud the place,
And all the forest huddled close with fear.
He turned around; Leona's face had fled,
But oh, the spectre there before his eyes!
For just a pace beyond him stood a shape
Whose awful presence curdled all his blood.
It was a woman with a sweeping robe
That shrouded her in ghastly spectral folds.
In her right hand she held a scorpion whip,
And in her left a leafy branch of ash.
Her face was livid, pale, and pinched and wan,
With burning eyes beneath her haggard brows,
Like fiery coals in gray volcanic cones.
He could not move, as though his limbs were stone,
His brow was damp with cold and clammy dews.

She gazed upon him sternly; then she said,
"Thyself shalt bring a curse upon thyself.
He who loves not another loves himself,
And he shall crave in vain to ease his soul;
True love drinks life-blood from another heart,
But selfish love doth gnaw upon his own.
Farewell! thy choice is made, and thou shalt find
In loving self thou graspest at a shade."

III.

She glided from him like a ghost of night,
And glimmered dimly through the branching boughs
Till lost to sight amid the forest gloom.

Narcissus shivered, for the breeze had chilled,
And trembling birds for fear had ceased to sing.
The nymphs, aroused, had fled before her face.
The startled, shuddering trees with horror moaned.
Like huddled cattle, when, on tainted air,
With horns erect, eyes starting, mad with fear,
And lowing, groaning deep and piteously,
From altar stones they smell their comrade's blood.

Again he turned and gazed into the brook,
And saw himself reflected in its waves.
Again he saw his sweet lips, glowing cheeks,
His azure eyes, his rippling golden hair,
His rounded, dimpled arms, his dainty feet,
And all the naked wonders of his form.
Then what a world of wistful agony

Came o'er his soul while gazing in the brook!
Oh, how he loved that shadow of himself!
Oh, how he longed to clasp it in his arms!
Oh, how he longed to kiss its rich red mouth!
What eager yearning swayed his bounding heart!
What flaming passion fired his leaping blood!
Such deep desire, such maddening thrills of love,—
A heaven of bliss, but just beyond his reach!
His pulses throbbing wildly to his head,
O'ercame him like a fierce, voluptuous dream.
He sought to kiss his own lips in dispair,
His own breast struggled vainly to embrace.
And then the deep eyes of the shadow there
Seemed begging him to share their languorous
    sweets.
Its lips seemed longing to be pressed to his,
Its arms inviting to their swoonful realm.

Filled with his pain, he could resist no more,
But leaped to clasp the shadow to his heart.
In vain, in vain! A splash, a chilly thrill,
And then the shadow fled before his eyes!
He struggled with the icy, mantling waves,
Clung to the bushy bank and climbed to shore,
But cold and shivering with the trickling drops.
Again he looked upon the cruel brook
That now had cursed him with his own fair face,
And once again he saw the shadow sweet
Gaze fondly at him from the mirror there.
No lover ever longed to clasp his love

With half such fervor as Narcissus did.
But yet, alas! that passion could be fed
On rounded beauties of the loved one's breast,
And lulled to sleep by blissful blandishments.
All others who have loved, with amorous play,
Have felt at last their passion satisfied,
Have drunk the bubbling cup of Cupid's joy,
And cooled the raging fever of desire.
But his love was a fire with naught to quench,
A sleepless craving that had naught to lull;
He hungered for a fruit he could not taste,
He thirsted for a cup he could not quaff.

The lover who hath not his love returned
Hath yet the sympathy of every heart,
Hath others, placed like him, to share his grief,
And feels ennobled by his sad, sweet pain.
The guilty lovers, scorned by all the world,
Still find a happier world within themselves.
But oh, the horror of unnatural love,
Beyond the sympathy of every soul!
With no one sharing in that agony,
His own cheeks seared with tears of baffled shame!

And then, again, he felt such agony
He leaped once more amid the brook's cold waves.
Ah, still in vain! A splash, a chilly thrill,
And once again the shape eluded him!
Then deep despair fell o'er him like a shroud,
And like a child, lost in the night, he sobbed.

The twilight, like a priestess, crowned with stars,
Draped Day's fair ringlets in the veil of night,
Stabbed his white bosom, lit his funeral pyre,
And with her victim died in crimson flames.
The swallow glided to his eave to sleep;
The wild dove fluttered to her peaceful nest;
The shepherd drove his thirsty flocks to drink,
Then led them, bleating, to their nightly fold;
The new moon, like a harvest sickle, shone
Through golden grains and flowers in fields of
    heaven;
The gentle shadows gathered in the woods,
And laid kind hands on Nature's dreaming soul;
But still Narcissus lay beside the brook,
Longing to perish with the hapless day,
Whose curse had pierced him with an agony
Unsoothed and cureless by the balms of night.

IV.

The weary days lagged on like crippled churls,
And sweet Narcissus withered in despair.
His blue eyes faded with their sleepless cares,
Like desert skies with parching fervor wan;
His crimson lips were mutely quivering
Like flaming dead leaves in the autumn winds;
His dimpled cheeks were pinched, and blanched
    and thin,
Like great white roses fading day by day;
His graceful step came to a weary halt
Like stiffened lameness of the wounded doe.

Hour after hour he gazed upon the brook,
And the big tears dropped in its azure waves.
But still he lived while ever loathing life,
And begging heaven to be allowed to die.
He gazed in anguish at the ghostly face
Which in despair looked up from depths below,
With great eyes mournful, outstreched bony hands
That beckoned to him like an aspen's leaves.

One day while lying on a bank of moss
He heard a rustle,—Echo's stealthy step.
"Narcissus!" said she sweetly in his ear;
He turned toward her, bursting into tears.
No longer did he seek to flee her face,
But longed to mingle bitter tears with hers.
"Narcissus," said she, "I shall share thy grief,
My woeful heart shall ever throb with thine.
Long have I watched thee, feared to come to thee,
But thou, I know, wilt never drive me hence.
Thy hopeless love consumes thine own sad heart,
And mine upon another's cast away;
Our souls are bound together by a bond
Of mutual, never-changing misery."
He wept, then laid his head upon her breast,
And soon with weeping lulled himself to sleep.

What bounding, leaping throbs of wild delight,
What dreamy, balmy, soothing spells of bliss,
Filled all her soul while clasping him to heart!
She softly smoothed his thin dishevelled locks,

And tenderly she stroked his pallid cheeks.
She would have given the treasures of the sea
For one soft pressure 'gainst that dreaming face,
And all the gold of all the tribes of earth
For one strong clasping of those tender arms,
And all the glories of the starry skies
For one warm kiss from that enchanting mouth,—
But she dared not for fear of waking him!
Ah, hapless hearts, that beat together now,
Yet parted by a universe of tears!
Ah, hapless souls, each craving for the same,
And each forever doomed to pine in vain!
Ah, would that Fate had bound them both together
Like bride and bridegroom on their nuptial night!

Soon through the woods was heard the bay of hounds,
And then the huntress nymph of Artemis
Came tripping down the pathway to the brook,
The hounds still yelping as she moved along.
Her naked breasts were heaving joyously
Like water-lilies on the rocking waves,
While silvery laughter fluttered on her lips.
Her right arm bore the skin of spotted pard
Torn warm and bleeding from the victim's back.
She oped her lips to cry out in delight,
And tell poor Echo of the morning's sport;
But Echo beckoned her to tread tiptoe,
And speak in whispers that he might not wake.

"Is this Narcissus?" asked the huntress maid:
"Oh, what a fearful, wasting change is here!

Once I beheld him like a milk-white fawn,
But stricken now and lying down to die;
Once I beheld him like a lotus flower,
The peerless swelling blossom wonderful,
Then budding in unearthly loveliness,
Now lying withered in the sultry dust;
Once I beheld him like the round, full moon,
In naked beauty rising on the night,
With mellow, golden glory in his orb,
O'er lovers true in odorous gardens sweet,
But now, as gaunt and haggard as its wane,
When hanging shattered, blanched and thin and wan,
Above the bare boughs of a blasted wood,
He sinks to perish in the Western wilds."

Poor Echo could not answer for her tears.
The huntress gazed in silence at the hounds
Laving their gray flanks in the crystal stream,
Lapping sweet waters with their jagged jaws,
And shaking dew-drops from their hanging ears.

Then said the huntress, starting, "I forgot,
In speaking of Narcissus' deep despair,
To tell thee that which surely brings thee joy.
Thou dost remember that, on yester-eve,
Down through the Western scarlet skies of flame
A spotless swan came fluttering to thy feet,
A cruel arrow rankling in his breast.
Then thou, with kind hands, didst remove the dart,

So that the swan arose and soared away.
Know thou that swan belonged to Artemis,
And she is grateful to thee, hapless nymph.
She bids me tell thee beg one boon of her,
Speak the one wish that lieth next thy heart,
And thou shall see at once thy dream come true."

Echo at first by this was so amazed
She scarce made answer to the kindly nymph,
But overjoyed, at last shed floods of tears,
Gave heartfelt thanks, and cried out in delight,
" Oh, I shall now to heavenly scenes return.
Long have I wandered through these earthly wilds,
And yearned again to see my happy home.
How often when chill autumn filled the skies
With dead leaves flying from the haggard trees,
How often when the winter winds on high
Bore flocks of cranes towards the Southern seas,
How often when the mortals passed me by
In funeral trains, with some enshrouded form,
How often, in those days, I craved for thee,
Olympus blest, free from decay and death!
I long to see thy banquet-halls again,
And take the ruby wine from Hebe's hands,
I long to see dear Iris smile once more,
And spend sweet converse on the days gone by,
To gaze on youthful Eros' face, and drink
Immortal glory from his wondrous eyes!"
But Fate would hearken not to Echo's prayer,
And gathered other woes to wound her soul,

For then Narcissus murmured in his dreams,
"Oh, would that I could die! but I can not;
The gods can not immortal life destroy.
Oh, would that heaven, in pity on my grief,
Might change me to some painless, dreamless
  flower!"

Echo seemed stricken with a deadly wound,
And then grew still and rigid as a stone.
A moment like a long age slowly passed,
And then she said, "Will kindly Artemis
Grant more than one wish unto hapless me?
May I return to heaven and save him too?"

"Alas!" the nymph cried; "it can never be;
For jealous Here hates thee, stricken maid.
My mistress scarce could gain consent from Zeus
Who hath betrayed thee to his furious queen,
To let thee have the granting of one wish,
And much great Here murmured when 'twas
  known
That this one favor was bestowed on thee.
Thou mayest choose to help Narcissus there,
But if thou dost, Olympus shalt not see.
The curse upon Narcissus can not die
As long as life remains within his breast,
And as he is immortal, he must change
His present shape, and live another life.
He must be buried as the mortals are,
And from his grave a flower will soon ascend

To take the life of him now in your arms.
But that would be a special boon of heaven,
And the great gods would do no more for thee."

"Oh, no!" cried Echo, "do not change his form!
How can I bear to see my precious love
Changed to the lifeless beauty of a plant?
Oh, spare him, spare him! pity, pity me!
'Twill bury me forever in despair!"

"But," said the other, "if he changeth not,
His soul must writhe in never-dying pain."

"Ah!" Echo cried, "shall I be doomed forever
On cheerless Earth to roam in banishment,
And nevermore behold Olympus blest?
Or must I, hapless maiden, doom my love
To sink forever in the dismal grave?
What countless ages shall I wander here,
To see earth wither in the myriad years,
Behold her cities ruined, desolate,
And generations pass away and die!
To think that I must tread those endless years,
Amid these deserts of decay and death,
Without my love, the idol of my soul,
And live, still live, alone, alone, alone!"
"Still," said the huntress, "he must either
    change
Or live a life of deathless agony."

"I love him," said poor Echo, shedding tears,—
"Let it be so: his good shall be my prayer!
I choose not to return to heaven with thee,
But beg thy mistress to relieve *his* woes!"
The huntress glided from her through the woods,
But heard behind the piteous sound of sobs;
Turned, and beheld sad Echo clasp her love
As some fond mother hugs her dying child,
Speak words of burning love within his ears,
Then kiss his sleeping face a thousand times;
And as the nymph towards Olympus soared,
She heard, blurred by the distance, many moans,
Till misty clouds obscured her view of earth,
And rushing winds stilled all its dreamy hum.

V.

Once more the morning, like a gorgeous rose
Bursts into blossom in a field of fire;
Once more her white steeds, shaking silvery manes,
Leap forth, caparisoned in blue and gold;
Once more her handmaids wreathe the clouds with
    flowers,
From crystal goblets sprinkle ruby wines;
Once more the pale moon in their veils of light
Is shrouded like a dead bride for the tomb;
Once more her sweet kiss thrills the dewy stars,
Till all those orbs celestial faint with love,
Then melt their glories on her milk-white breasts,
And perish in the splendor of her hair.

But as the light fell on Narcissus' brow
Its rosy flame tinged livid hues of death.
The dryads swung amid the leafy boughs,
The water-nymphs arose above the waves,
The sylphs flew round like jeweled butterflies,
And zephyrs hummed like golden-wingéd bees.
But Echo heeded not those beauteous forms,
And saw naught save her loved one dying there.

His head lay pillowed on her tender breast
Beneath the shadow of a hoary oak,
His breath was coming slower, slower still,
His eyes were ever growing dim and dark.
He had been told how Artemis had given
This one boon to her lonely, aching heart.
Oft had he thanked her for remembering him,
But never thought what sacrifice she made.
Alas! how often doth unselfish love
See all its tears unnoticed or forgot!
"One boon I beg," sobbed Echo, timidly;
"Wilt thou kiss me, my love, before thou diest?"
He put his thin white arms around her neck,
And faintly smiled upon her pallid face;
He held his fevered, quivering lips to hers,
And fell back fainting in her trembling arms;
Then, sinking slowly, bowed his golden head,
And with one lingering, piteous moan, he died.

A curdling cry pierced through the startled air,
And woful Echo clasped a leaden corpse.

The pensive Evening trod the Western hills,
Her saffron mantle glowing in the skies
Like yellow foliage of the autumn woods.
Through silent dells and lonely mountain groves
Her dusky shades, like mourners, crept along.
Then all the shepherds of the neighboring vales,
And all the lovely mortal maidens there,
Came gathering round to look into his face,
Soon to be hid beneath the chilly clods.
And maiden hands brought many a beauteous flower
To scatter o'er his sad, untimely grave,
White, azure, pink and purple hyacinths,
With valley-lilies, frail and delicate,
And crocus-bloosoms, pansies rich and dark.
Soft buttercups and creamy daffodils,
The modest white and purple violets,
New-opened daisies, with their hearts of gold,
Sweet cowslips, and primroses gemmed with dew.
But he was lovelier than those beauteous buds,
And sweeter than their faint and odorous breath.
His pearly eyelids, closed for evermore,
Now hid the azure of his dreaming eyes;
His pallid cheeks lay slumbering calm and still;
The tiny dimples slept around his mouth;
His soft white hands were folded on his heart,
Like two sweet doves dead in one little nest;
Pure water-lilies wreathed his golden hair,
And rich musk-roses bloomed above his breast.

They buried him in damp and cheerless earth,
To be the prey of death's corrupting hand,

And every clod that fell upon him there
Dropped like a mountain on poor Echo's heart.

Months passed away, and then a pallid plant
Arose and blossomed on his lonely grave;
His soul had passed within that tender flower,
And even now it bears Narcissus' name.

Then Echo glided from the sight of men,
And wandered through the trackless wilderness,
Through lonely valleys, mountains high and still,
Forever weeping, calling out his name.
She pined away, grew pale and paler still,
Then flitted like the shadow of a curse,
Until at last her voice alone was left
To answer vaguely every vagrant sound.
Great nations perish, but she can not die;
Vast empires crumble, but she lingers still.
The gray gods in Olympus' lofty halls
From jeweled goblets quaff their nectar still;
She, unforgiven, never can return,
Her name forgotten by them long ago.
And so she wanders ever, suffering still
Undying anguish and undying love.

1887.

THE MENDELSSOHN WEDDING MARCH.

I AM standing mutely hearkening to thy passion-pealing notes
Soaring like a thousand songsters trilling with triumphant throats;

Sweet as mellow strains a-floating from the huntsman's bugle-horn
Far amid the verdant mountains, through the crimson skies of morn;

Thrilling like the trump of battle, when its peals arising high
Rouse the dormant soul to rapture, calling men to bleed and die.

And the joyous lover hearkens to those blissful, blissful strains,
Till his heart soars like an eagle, tearing from his captor's chains;

Sweet to him as songs of seraphs, in a dying pilgrim's ear,
As he sees the earth grow dimmer and the pearly gates draw near!

But, his hapless rival listens with a furious, fierce despair
And his heart leaps like a lion in his grim and gloomy lair;

And he hearkens to its echoes as a corpse within the tomb
Hears the distant rumbling thunder of the judgement trump of doom.

Still **resounding**, still **resounding**, are those wild and wondrous peals,
Till a maze of weird enchantment far around the spirit steals.

Ah, what dreams of bliss celestial, ah, what throngs of waking woes!
Ah, what dreams of summer splendors, ah, what storms of winter snows!

Ah, how many feet have trodden to that music rich and rare,
Some bewinged with blissful blessings, others weighted with despair!

Some to love's enchanted empire, mystic isles of blissful bloom,
Some to hatred's blasted kingdom, shrouded in eternal gloom;

Some with trustful eyes adoring, casting all but love away,
Some betraying love for riches, trampling heart and soul in clay;

Some to live a life triumphant, loving, loyal, bright and brave,
Some to see hope lost forever, sinking in a living grave!

"THE LOVE OF WOMAN."

THE love of Woman blends within its spell,
    The noon-day glory and the gloom of night,
The smiles of angels, frowns of demons fell,
    The summer splendor and the autumn blight.

Her love is like a richly jeweled mine
    With starry gems in burnished skies of gold,
Or devious cavern, where no sun may shine,
    Whose strange, sad secrets tongue hath never told.

It sways the heart-strings like a seraph's hymn
    Resounding softly through the vesper sky;
Or like a witch's song in forest dim,
    Which lures the traveler to her feet to die.

It thrills man's bosom like a nectar rare,
    Till, like a God, he soars on wings of flame,
Or like a poisoned wine, with baleful snare,
    Which hurls him reeling in the mire of shame.

Her love is like a sacred asphodel
    Which blossoms in the realms of deathless day,
Or lotus, numbing heroes by its spell,
    Till honor, fame and courage pass away.

Her love hath lifted man to godlike joy,
    As Cynthia led Endymion to the skies,
Or like false Helen, firing towers of Troy,
    Hath smote him with the splendor of her eyes.

She binds him with a wondrous witching wile
    To give his life to anguish or to bliss,
To win his soul's salvation with a smile,
    Or slay his hopes of heaven with a kiss.

"AS MORNING COMES."

AS Morning comes, to scatter through the skies
    The dewy lilies from her wings of white,
And greets the noontide with her sparkling eyes,
    Then sinks to perish in the solemn night;

As Springtime comes in laughter and in joy,
    Then blossoms into summer rich and rare,
Till autumn blasts her garlands green destroy
    And winter shrouds her in his chill despair;

As Childhood comes in brilliance and bloom,
    And gathers glory with the fleeting years,
Then flutters like a dead leaf to his doom,
    Amid a storm of sobbing and of tears;

So young Love came, mine aching heart to soothe,
    And so I gladly took him in my door,
My Morning and my Springtime and my Youth,
    And so he left me, sad for evermore.

BETROTHED.

THOU hast my heart, and thou shall have my hand,
 Thy captive shall not crave her freedom more;
 Wert thou an exile on a desert shore,
For thee my feet should leave their native land;
If on thy brow were Cain's accurséd brand,
 Thee as a white-robed saint would I adore;
 Wert thou my master, I in bondage sore
Would rather serve thee than a realm command.

Yet know, as thou art true or false to me
 My life shall pass in glory or in gloom;
Thy nuptial vow unto my heart shall be
 A song of triumph or a trump of doom;
Thy bosom, Love, to which my soul doth flee,
 A couch of roses, or a living tomb.

A GIFT.

I SEND a spray of roses, decked with dew,
   And robed in richest red and white attire,
To tell the story of my love for you
   With souls of splendor and with hearts of fire.

The eager red rose flushes fervently,
   The timid white rose faintly breathes my name;
One flower of passion, one of purity,
   A star of snowflake and a star of flame.

And you may kiss them, in their morning glow;
   When passion pulses in their fresh perfume
From lips of ruby and from lips of snow
   In all the glory of their blissful bloom.

But when their beauteous bosoms all are brown,
   And silken leaflets all are drooped and dry,
Your hands will fling my fading roses down
   And you will leave them in the dust to die.

And so I give my fervant heart to you
   To please your fancy through a fleeting day;
And then you weary of its passion true,
   And ca st it lightly in the dust away.

"TO ONE WHO WILL UNDERSTAND."

MY secret I have whispered in thine ears;
 To none but thee, my love, the truth is known;
The world is listening, but it never hears
 The sweet confessions made to thee alone.

They know not if thy face be dark or fair,
 A pearly lily or a queenly rose,
Or if thy cheeks the stronger semblance bear
 To summer sunsets or to winter snows.

They know not, darling, if thine eyes are blue
 Or brown as tropic twilights, precious love,
Or black as berries decked with diamond dew,
 Or like the gray wings of a dreaming dove;

Or if the tresses which thy face enfold
 Are like the bronze-brown of a hazel husk
A sable shadow, or a crown of gold,
 Or like the auburn of an autumn dusk.

Yet, dearest, as the blossom to the bee,
 Or listening maiden to the lover's lute,
So, precious, thou shalt ever be to me,
 My heart's own treasure, and its flower and fruit.

"I LOVE THY FAULTS."

I LOVE thy faults. If angels said to me:
    " We give thee power to change her at thy will,"
My heart, forever loyal unto thee,
    Would leave thee as thou art, my darling, still.

If, like a sculptor in the days of old,
    My hands might mould a form and face divine,
Mine eyes would turn from all their beauty cold,
    And see no sweet face in the world but thine.

If I should tread through blest abodes above,
    And win the love of angels wondrous fair,
My soul would loathe their chill perfection, love
    And then return, thy lowly lot to share.

If thou hast faults, my creed shall make them right;
    I love thee only and I ever will.
If thou art lowly, yet thy hut is bright—
    If heaven disown thee, I shall claim thee still.

L'AMANTE DU DIABLE.

"Woman wailing for her Demon Lover"
       COLERIDGE.

ALL around me, in the darkness, monstrous mountain ridges stand,
Guarding all the haunted pathways to this dim, enchanted land·

In the west I see the tatters of the dull and drooping clouds,
Where the faded sunset glories slumber in their gloomy shrouds;

And I see the moon's frail crescent near a dewy, diamond star,
Shining from the gates celestial, where the saints and seraphs are;

But a mighty tempest gathers in the perished twilight's path
As a shaggy lion rises, trembling with his awful wrath;

And the lightnings flash and quiver like the scorpion lashes' stings
Drawing blood from cheeks of demons, flying with their routed kings;

While the thunder peals gigantic far across the cliffs
    are hurled,
Crashing like a mighty planet on a wrecked and
    ruined world;

And the winds, aroused and startled, moaning in
    in their frantic flight,
Fill my soul with sad foreboding on this horror-
    haunted night.

Once two brothers, deadly foemen, met upon this
    wrinkled wold,
And within each other's bosoms drove their daggers
    keen and cold:

And a pair of guilty lovers, hiding in this place of
    woe,
At the stake were burned to ashes in the dim years
    long ago;

And a traitor seeking refuge when this ancient land
    was young,
By a throng of furious yeomen on this withered
    tree was hung.

Here I come to meet thee, Satan, ruined king
    whom I adore,
Thou, my prince, my lord, my master, and my
    monarch evermore!

Now I see thee come to meet me and I rush within
    thine arms,
While my bosom bounds with passion for thy wild
    and wondrous charms.

I, the seraph, blest and beauteous, robed in radiant
    starry light,
With my golden locks encircled with the pearly
    lilies white,

I, that soar on swan-like pinions, blossom-bosomed,
    flower-fair,
I, with eyes like purest dew-drops, twinkling in
    the azure air,

I have come to meet thee, Satan, with thy wings
    of ashen gray,
Seared with sins and seared with sorrows that shall
    never pass away!

With thine eyes so grand and gloomy, raven tres-
    ses flecked with frost,
And thy mien so melancholy, hapless Monarch of
    the Lost!

With thy step so proud and princely, as it seems
    to spurn the sod,
With thy high brow, scarred and blasted by the
    cruel bolts of God!

I have left the vine-clad vistas and the palms of paradise,
Where the song-birds sing forever under diamond-tinted skies,

Where the silken, saffron roses swoon with odors rich as wine,
And the sprays of jasmine blossoms through the myrtle branches twine,

Where the crystal fountains bubble under woods forever green,
And the fields are gemmed with glories like a gorgeous Eastern queen,—

Left them all to meet thee, Satan,—left my throne and crown and lyre,
Flying through the myriad systems, past the whirling stars of fire!

Satan, grander than the mountains, with their gloomy giant forms!
Satan, grander then the heavens, with their wild, majestic storms!

Satan, grander than the ocean, with its vast and solemn waves!
Satan, grander than the desert, with its withered waste of graves!

Like a fierce volcano rising with its regal crimson crest!
Like a wierd and wondrous comet, terrifying every breast!

Let me heal thy wounded visage where the jagged lightnings fell,
Kiss thy worn feet, burned and blackened by the flaming dust of Hell!

I have angel wooers, Satan, who can never win my love,
For my heart was hurled to Hades when they hurled thee from above;

And those angel lovers, Satan, all are grand, divinely fair,
With their gray eyes soft and saintly, with their waving golden hair·

With their princely eagle pinions, sandals flecked with sparkling gems,
And their broad white brows majestic, wreathed with starry diadems

With their voices sweet and solemn, like the poet kings of old,
As they stand before the Master with their wondrous harps of gold.

And they sing me songs of passion, melting from their lips divine,
And around my clustered ringlets purple lotus blossoms twine.

But I turn from angel faces, come to cheer thee in thy doom,
Kiss the wan, wild star thou wearest in thy forehead's mournful gloom;

So I steal from heights of heaven and the realms of deathless day,
Meet thee in benighted deserts in this lone world far away,

Or I wander till I find thee, flying on from zone to zone,
And I throw mine arms around thee on thine ever-burning throne.

THE POTTERS FIELD

I.

SEE the lonesome fields forsaken in their desolation spread,
Heaving with the silent grave-mounds of the nameless pauper dead.

Never blooms a rose above them, never peeps a violet here,
No one comes to sit beside them, no one comes to shed a tear.

No one speaks a word of pity, no one breathes a word of love,
Earth around them shrinks with loathing, heaven recoils with scorn above.

Here are sleeping thieves and beggars, here the outcast babes of shame,
Here the felon from the gallows, here the waif without a name.

Here the suicide lies sleeping, with the madman by his side
And the drunkard and the spendthrift in the same strange home abide.

Here the ruined woman slumbers, while her lover, far away
In his revels, thinketh never of his victim in the clay.

Yet what vernal visions wreathed them in their childhood long ago!
Ah, what aspirations perished in the pauper graveyard low!

Ah, what happy mothers kissed them in their lovely boyish bloom,
Never dreaming that their idols thus should share the felon's tomb!

Ah, what trustful maidens kissed them, gazing in their eyes so brave,
Never dreaming that their lovers thus should share the drunkard's grave!

And the ardent lover fondling this frail outcast's golden hair,
Never dreamed that he, a traitor, should thus drive her to despair,

Nor that this same trustful being, burning with a love untold,
Soon would sink and lie decaying in the pauper graveyard mould.

While their babe, scorned and deserted, soon
    would hide his shameful birth
Far below in dust polluted of the pauper grave-
    yard's earth.

II.

But amid the nameless outcasts sleep the good and
    brave and true,
They who lived and died for duty, they the world's
    immortal few.

For the palm to those deserving evermore shall be
    denied;
They must tread the earth with beggars, slumber
    by the beggars' side;

And the good and great and noble in a lowly grave
    lie down
Ere the fickle world rewards them with the sceptre
    and the crown.

Here are sleeping peerless poets, they who
    begged from door to door,
But whom Death has wreathed with laurels green
    and glad forevermore!

Here are sleeping brave old martyrs, they who
    strove to make us free,
Whom the flames consumed to ashes for their love
    of you and me.

And they sleep as sweetly, calmly, in these pauper graveyard scenes,
As the laurelled victor slumbers by the side of kings and queens.

Here are sleeping countless heroes, whom the world remembers not,
They who loved and toiled and struggied in their chill and cheerless lot;

But while Earth has turned unheeding in its hurried stir and strife,
Angels all their names have treasured in the Master's book of life!

III.

Now I dream I see the dawning of the awful judgment day,
Far across the Eastern mountains, and the Eastern seas away.

And the dull ears of those sleepers hear the trumpet in their palls,
While their dumb tongues strive to answer to its wild, soul-stirring calls.

And from out their rusted coffins myriad bony shapes arise,
While their dim eyes catch the glimmer in the vast, vague eastern skies.

Then the beggar feebly totters from his grim and gaping grave,
And he stands at last the equal of the great and strong and brave;

Then the felon struggles slowly from his dark and dusty shroud,
There to face the last of Judges with the rich and high and proud;

Then the ruined woman rises with her infant from the tomb,
There to meet her trembling lover who at last must share her doom.

So the pauper graveyard's children unto endless life arise,
Now the equal of the haughty in the great Creator's eyes;

Still to live and live forever, when the myriad years have fled,
When the world is crushed to atoms, and the suns and stars are dead.

TEMPTED.

WILT thou feel no pang of pity as I turn with tears to thee?
Ah, desist, thou darling Tempter, loose thy grasp and set me free

In thine eyes I see the fury and the frenzy of desire,
Till my pulses thrill my bosom and my heart and soul with fire.

So I dare not spurn or scorn thee, so my poor feet can not fly,
And my soul is filled with longing in thine eager arms to die.

As the sparrow sees the serpent coiling close around her nest
Till the spellbound mother flutters fainting on his jeweled crest:

As the terror-stricken traveler in the desert's devious ways
Sees a tiger crouch before him with his cruel eyes ablaze:

As the fated youth sits gazing at the goblet's purple rim
And beholds his wreck and ruin rising in the future dim:

As the numb, enchanted dreamer sees the nightmare drawing near
When his tongue is dumb with horror and his feet are chained with fear:

So I see thee, sweetest Tempter, snare me in thy fearful charms
While I dare not shrink or struggle, but must sink within thine arms.

Ah, what joy, what bliss enchanting, soon to droop with blast and blight!
Ah, what brilliant blooms of morning, soon to perish in the night!

Now Remorse is faintly calling, dimly calling in mine ears,
Far away from days of childhood, far away through realms of tears!

As the horn of Roland sounded, far across the mounts and vales,
While his comrades, leagues beyond him, faintly heard its piteous wails;

As his myriad foemen slew him when no comrade's aid was nigh,
So Remorse, at bay, surrounded, soon must fall to dust, and die.

Now I see far in the future gathering hosts of deathless woes,
See my springtime blossoms perish in the chill white winter snows;

See my old friends all forsake me, see them laugh to hear my name,
See my mother's piercing anguish, see my father curse my shame,

See me sinking, lower, lower, sinking, sinking lower down,
In the night-time, homeless, friendless, wandering through the wicked town.

And I see thee, cruel Tempter, laughing at my loving trust;
See thee turn the traitor, Tempter, see thee hurl me in the dust.

But thy fearful fascination chains me in thine eager arms,
And I strive in vain to rouse me from thy fell and fateful charms.

So I turn from all the glories of the blest abodes above,
That my soul may share the blisses of thy baleful, blasting love.

So I turn from home and hearthstone, father, mother, comrades, all,
So I cease to struggle, Tempter, and I waver, and I fall.

THE RESURRECTION.

I HAVE watched and I have waited through the flight of months and years,
I have watched and I have waited through a world of doubts and fears.

Loving you through vernal vistas, when the Easter lily blows,
Loving you through chill Decembers with their swirls of silent snows;

Loving you through stately Summers, with their wealth of golden sheaves,
Loving you through mournful Autumns, with their crowns of withered leaves;

Loving you amid the shadows of the melancholy night,
Loving you amid the carols of the birds at morning light.

But I lost you, and I heeded not their glory or their gloom,
For my loyal heart was buried in the shadow of the tomb;

And it crumbled in its charnel where the bolts of iron rust,
Prisoned under walls of granite in the ashes and the dust;

The Resurrection.

Far away in haunted deserts, over solemn seas forlorn,
Far beyond the mystic mountains, never lit by light of morn:

In a realm of mournful midnight, where no friendly feet may tread,
Shrouded with the silent sleepers, in the dwellings of the dead.

But I heard you calling, Darling, through the bitterness and blight,
Through the death and desolation, through the dark December night.

And the charnel bolts were broken, and a Seraph set me free,
As the angel came at midnight to the tomb in Galilee.

Once again I feel the fervor of the swoonful springtime flowers,
Once again I see the brilliance of the summer's blissful bowers.

Once again the brooklets bubble and I see the happy herds:
Once again I hear the trilling of a thousand blithesome birds.

All is mirthful, all is merry, earth and sea and sky above;
And the bees and buds and breezes all are telling tales of love.

And my hands shall scatter roses, arch her path with garlands green,
For my loyal heart is longing for the coming of the Queen.

She is coming, and shall never leave her love to tread alone;
Coming back to reign forever, to her scepter and her throne!

She is coming, she is coming! all is grand and all is glorious,
She is coming, she is coming! and my heart is now victorious!

So her sweet face close beside me, shall be banished from me never;
And the night of desolation fadeth from my heart forever.

SEPARATED.

I SAW a thousand faces on my way,
    But I was lonely, for thou wert not there!
I missed the glory of thy golden hair,
And sought thy sweet face all the dreary day,
As through the haunts of songsters soft in May,
Some sad bird seeks his mate in dumb despair,
Or through the skies, where countless torches glare,
A lost star seeks its own sun's friendly ray.

Mayhap thy soul doth long my soul to greet,
Mayhap thy lips my fervent kisses crave;
But we no more upon one path may meet,
Than if between us spread the wold and wave;
So darling, in thy bosom soft and sweet
My love hath found its cradle and its grave.

FORTUNE TELLING.

WHEREVER you go, my brave little boy,
    With bluest of eyes and brightest of hair,
With laughter and love and jesting and joy,
    So free from the stains of earthly despair,
I know that some day you too shall shed tears,
    Shall drink of a cup of wormwood and gall;
Shall fade like a leaf in the flight of the years,
    Till coffin and shroud shall cover it all,—
Wherever you go, my darling,
                   Wherever you go.

Wherever you go, my brave little man,
    Your poor little feet shall falter at last,
Your hopes shall deceive, strive on as you can,
    And hope shall become a thing of the past:
Your heart shall be seared with shame and with sin,
    And bleed as you think of innocence fled;
The day shall depart and night shall begin,
    When Beauty and Youth and Pleasure are dead,—
Wherever you go, my darling,
                   Wherever you go.

Wherever you go, my darling, my dear,
    Beside you I see a shadow forlorn,
A phantom of sin and sorrow and fear,—
    The man you shall be in years to be born.

Fortune Telling.

I know not, my boy, if you shall win fame,
   If Fortune shall give you a chain or a crown;
No matter, my boy, it still is the same;
   The flower must fade, the ship must go down,—
Wherever you go, my darling,
                    Wherever you go.

"I WONDER WHY."

I WONDER why our sweetest joys are sins,
    Why Pleasure treadeth hand in hand with Death,
Why Beauty bloometh with a poisoned breath,
    Why burning Love and blasting Hate are twins,
    Why Passion stingeth when its bliss begins,
Why adders coil around the wine-cup's wreath
And why the flaming sword leaps from its sheath
    To slay him who the fruit forbidden wins.

For Love and Youth and Beauty thou shalt see,
    Reeling with wine in swoonful sweetness lie
Beneath a green-boughed, golden-fruited tree,
    While Hatred, Death and Madness crouch near by.
O, tempted traveler, turn and quickly flee!
    For if thou pluckest, thou shalt surely die.

LIFE.

I SAW a throng of prisoners in a cell,
   Who, one and all, were doomed to die next day.
  Some laughed and shouted in a reckless way,
Some raved and cursed and swore like demons fell,
Some sobbed and bade their friends a last farewell,
   Some shuddered in a dream of dull dismay,
   Some ate, some drank, or sat with cards at play,
Some seemed to hearken to a funeral bell.

Mine eyes with pity for them filled with tears;
   But they are living just as you and I.
The prison is this world of fitful fears,
   The prisoners but our doomed humanity;
Our day is set within a few short years,
   And laugh, or weep, or curse, like them we die.

"I KNOW NOT WHY I LOVE THEE."

I KNOW not why I love thee. There may be
  A thousand fairer, wiser; yet I pine
    O precious Love, alone to call thee mine.
One life, one love is given unto me,
One life, one love is given unto thee;
    One fleeting day we drink this cup divine,
    One fleeting day thine arms around me twine,
And then we slumber through eternity.

If I may win thee, all is deathless day;
    Hope's brilliant banners never shall be furled;
If I may win thee, grief shall pass away,
    And every anguish in the dust be hurled.
If I must lose thee, all is crumbling clay,—
    I lose my soul, my lifetime, all the world.

THE REDBIRD.

Redbird, Redbird, brave and brilliant, flitting on thy wings of flame,
Tell me, Redbird, shrill and startling, whence thy blood-red plumage came?

Like a scarlet-crested poppy, blazing in the sultry noon,
Like the frail, enchanted crescent of the crimson setting moon;

Like a spray of fiery tulips, with their hearts of golden light,
Like a ruby star arising in the shadows of the night;

Like the burning blush of sunrise, in the eastern skies away,
Like the sunset's splash of splendor from the bleeding heart of day;

Flaming through the dogwood blossoms, creamy-clustered locust trees,
Swinging on the grape-vine's tendrils, flying with the booming bees;

Mingling with the scarlet trumpets, where the verdant creepers twine,
Flushing like a falling goblet, spilling out its sparkling wine;

Blushing through the cypress branches, through the green swamps, cool and still,
Waking all the emerald shadows with thy sharp and sudden trill;

Redbird, Redbird, brave and brilliant, flitting on thy wings of flame,
Tell me Redbird, shrill and startling, whence thy blood-red plumage came?

II.

I was once an Indian maiden, in the dream-years, long ago,
When the Redman in these forests first beheld his pale-faced foe.

Then a young knight with his comrades marched within our fatherland;
Never had our simple people seen so bright and brave a band;

And their leader trod before them, with a gay and gallant air,
With his blue eyes, dark and dreamy, with his clustered golden hair;

With his sweet mouth, like wild rose, and his cheeks
    of boyish bloom,
With his white brow overshadowed by his helmet's
    snowy plume.

All my people bade him welcome, though their
    hearts were hot with hate,
And they gave their hands in friendship, but in
    secret planned his fate.

Yet I often met the stranger, and he kindly spake
    to me
In the strange and broken accents of his home be-
    yond the sea;

And I often wandered with him, through the
    forest, field and dell,
And his sweet and subtle whispers bound me with
    a blissful spell.

I would tell him mystic legends of our tribe in
    vanished days,
Names of birds and trees and insects, blossoms
    budding in our ways,

Habits of the crawling serpent, cunning of the
    crafty fox,
Of the hare and hawk and squirrel, and the eagle
    in the rocks;

He would tell me of his people in the realms beyond the sea,
Of their kingdoms and their cities, like a wonderland to me.

So my soul was made his captive, and I longed to follow him,
As a slave beside her master, far beyond the mountains dim.

Once I stole among our chieftains, slipping like a stealthy spy,
And I heard the painted warriors swearing that my knight must die.

Then, with bare feet, in the midnight, through the dank and chilling dew,
Crawling, cringing, creeping, running, stole the silent village through:

Then I found my lover sleeping in his quiet tent, near by,
And revealed to him the secret, that he might not stay and die;

Then I pressed his bounding bosom to my palpitating breast,
Felt his fond farewell embraces, nevermore to be caressed;

Then I blessed him and I kissed him, to our village took my flight,
And I lost my love forever, on that anguish-haunted night.

And he fled from out our forests, baffled all the Indians' hate,
But he left me with my people,—left me there to meet my fate.

For the warriors knew me guilty, led me to a lonely wood,
And they stabbed mine aching bosom, till I perished, dyed in blood.

But my lover, false and fickle, never dreamed or cared for me,
Wooed and won a beauteous maiden in his home beyond the sea.

So my ghost is flitting ever, like an autumn leaflet red,
When the summer suns have faded, and the summer blooms have fled.

So I strive to hide my sorrow, as I flit from tree to tree,
As the cynic hides his anguish with a hollow-hearted glee.

So a woman's love, once given, nevermore shall pass away;
But the jewel, by her lover, soon is trampled in the clay.

THE CAPTIVE MOCKING-BIRD.

I SEE the mock-bird in his lonely cage,
   Forever banished from his native hills,
Still beating at his bars in helpless rage,
   And panting for the woodlands and the rills.

Yet, like the violin, which weaves in one,
   All other measures and all other notes,
He blends the songs sung under every sun
   With all the fervor of a thousand throats.

He sings the stanzas in his soul's distress
   Of all the poets ever known before,
The Shakespeare of the Western wilderness
   Who warbles lays of every sea and shore.

Ane like the highborn maidens long ago,
   Whose beauty brought a dowry of despair,
Or ancient minstrels, with their lives of woe,
   Forever doomed to want and wasting care,

His soaring spirit clanks its cruel chains,
   And strives and struggles in its hopeless rage:
His glorious gifts shall bring him burning pains,
   And only death can free him from his cage.

So, I remember, when a happy boy
   I roamed through fields and forests all abloom,
And by my side were Beauty and Love and Joy,
   Who soon departed to their silent tomb;

And I remember in those distant days,
   They brought me from my far-off happy home,
Sweet isles of Eden, lost in mellow maze
   Beyond the waste of ocean's flakes of foam.

And so my soul, with aspirations grand,
   On wings of song is seeking still to soar,
An exile in a strange and distant land
   Who sighs for splendors lost forevermore.

THE REVELLERS.

COME, my comrades, fill the glasses till they bubble to the brim,
For the hateful light of morning struggles through the shadows dim,

Like a witch's seething caldron on the hilltops of the East,
And I loathe it as it flickers on the ruins of our feast:

And I shudder as it glimmers with its flitting flames of blue,
Through the murky mists and mazes, through the cold and clammy dew.

Now we see each other's faces after all our fierce carouse,
Throbbing pulses, parching eyelids, flaming cheeks and haggard brows;

Now Remorse and Grief and Anguish come with stealthy, silent tread,
And our souls are writhing serpents, and our hearts are lumps of lead.

So, my comrades, fill the glasses, and our woes shall pass away;
We shall hide the wrecks and ruins scattered in the light of day.

And I see the glasses bubble with a splendor crystalline,
And I see them bubble, bubble, with a bounding bliss divine.

And I see them palpitating like the sparkling stars of night,
Like the ambient eyes of seraphs under foamy wings of white;

Here the red wine flames and flushes like the rose's burning breast,
Here the white wine shines and shimmers, like the lily's creamy crest;

Here the ruddy goblet glimmers like the glow of morning hours,
And the trembling white wine twinkles like the dews on spotless flowers.

Now I see the hazy hillsides of a land renowned in story,
Sung by sweetest songs of poets, decked in never-dying glory;

And I see the verdant vineyards in that wondrous kingdom old,
With their grapes of royal purple, and their clustered grapes of gold;

And I see the peasant maidens plucking from the loaded vines,
And I see their naked bosoms sweeter than delicious wines.

So I fly to lands of fancy, fearing to return to earth,
Strewn with wrecks and strewn with ruins, desert realms of death and dearth.

I have lost my youth forever, lost my honor and my name,
Trod the wastes of desolation, staggered through the mires of shame;

Once a sweet girl made me happy, as her blue eyes gazed in mine,
And her gentle smiles and kisses filled me with a love divine,

But the demon Dissipation tore the lovers far apart,
And her sweet face faded from me,—left me with a broken heart;

So at last the goblet's poison through my sense and spirit stole,
Till it owned my very being, and my body and my soul.

It has fettered me forever, and will never set me free;
It is mother, father, brother, sister, lover unto me.

Comrades, comrades, fill the glasses till the bright beads bubble o'er:
Drink to vanished dreams and visions, hopes now fled forevermore;

Drink to wrecks of time and talent, happy moments passed away,
Drink to ruined lives and labors, doomed to perish and decay;

Let the crystal glasses bubble, mocking at the morning light,
As we drink to desolation, coffin, shroud and endless night.

OUT OF THE FOLD.

ONE is astray from the Shepherd's fold,
    One is astray on the mountains cold,
Treading alone through the fading light,
Treading alone through the coming night.

And the Shepherd calls in his sweet, wild way,
Through the dreary dusk of the dying day,
Through the falling dews and the misty gloam,
For the one poor sheep that has strayed from home;

Weary and worn, with a piteous cry,
Weary and worn, he is sinking to die,
While the gaunt, gray wolves through the deserts dark,
Follow him fast with their fearful bark.

Will the Shepherd bear on his bosom warm
The wounded sheep from hurt and from harm?
Shall the poor lost lamb be left to his fate?
Shall the Shepherd come too late, too late?

    *   *   *   *   *

So runneth the story so sweet and so old
Of the sheep astray in the mountains cold,

Treading alone at dusk to his doom,
While the Shepherd calls through the gathering
    gloom.

So I am treading in piteous plight
Through the grief and gloom, through the coming
    night,
Treading the streets of the wicked town,
Treading the streets when the sun goes down.

Bearing a breast all burdened with woes
Through the biting winds and the bitter snows,
Suppressing a sob and choking a cry,
Hopeless of rest, yet fearing to die.

I have scoffed and scorned to smother my fears,
I have laughed aloud at thy streaming tears,
I have sung gay songs and quaffed of the wine
To forget thy face with its love divine.

Where the red light glares like an eye of fire,
In a gaudy room and in gay attire,
In the poisoned air, like a dragon's breath,
I stand at the stairs of the halls of death.

But behold, at my door the Sheperd stands,
And beckons to me with his bleeding hands,
And I see his feet all weary and worn,
His wounded breast and His crown of thorn!

Merciful Christ, with the princely grace,
Merciful Christ, with the sad, sweet face,
Merciful Christ, with the mournful eyes,
Remember me when the daylight dies!

Merciful Christ, thou hast followed afar
Under midnight moon, under evening star,
Treading with tears through forest and flood,
And tracing thy path with the stains of blood.

Merciful Christ, thou hast sought me here,
Through the mountains cold and the deserts drear;
Merciful Christ, am I left to my fate?
Merciful Christ, hast thou come too late?

I have heard thy voice as I passed along
Through the reveller's shout and the siren's song,
Through laughter, through fall of the dancing feet,
And the wicked jests of the crowded street;

But I perish alone in shame and in sin,
Though I long to arise and welcome thee in.
Merciful Christ, I cry unto thee,
Merciful Christ, have pity on me!

But the revellers riot, and the lewd songs swell,
And they numb my soul like a funeral knell;
In the noisy night, with its glitter and glare,
I wring my hands in my dark despair.

And I turn to thee in my dumb dismay,
As the demons cry like the wolves for prey;
Merciful Christ, shall thy feet depart
And leave me alone with my broken heart?

O Shepherd, come with thy footsteps fleet,
With my falling tears I shall wash thy feet,
And thy love shall lave my stains of despair,
As I wipe them dry with my streaming hair.

"WHEN THOU ART NEAR."

WHEN thou art near, when thou art near!
    Life seems so sweet beside thee, dear.
I seem to touch an angel's wing,
I feel her arms around me cling;
Within my heart a lily blooms
And glimmers through the mournful glooms;
Peace, like a white dove, nestles there,
And soothes my deep and dumb despair,
              When thou art near.

But when, O Love, thou art not near,
I shudder with a nameless fear;
I sit my lonely hearth beside,
Where anguish and despair abide;
I ponder in the solemn gloom
And tremble at some coming doom,
I feel Temptation stealing nigh,
While Sin and Sorrow hover by,
              And thou not near!

When thou art near, when thou art near!
Return and save, O save me, dear!
Thou knowest I am weak indeed,
And how thy helping hand I need.

See how the shadows gather near,
And beckon thee to leave me, dear!
O come to me, refuse me not!
Then I may bless my hapless lot
          When thou art near,
                    When thou art near!

"TO ONE WHO SHALL BE NAMELESS."

DO you sometimes think, as you pass me by,
   That I follow your steps with a stifled sigh?
Do you sometimes think, as you fade from view,
That my heart is broken for loss of you?

Will you think of me when the autumn blight
Shall sully my soul in the long years' flight,
When over my life, with its weight of woes,
Shall flutter the flakes of the winter snows?

Will you think of me in the fading light,
Will you think of me in the solemn night,
When the songs of spring and the summer blooms
All are asleep in their silent tombs?

Will you think of me when my hopes have fled,
Will you think of me when my heart is dead,
Will you think of me when my locks are gray,
And the light of my life has passed away?

Will you think of me when the azure skies
Are shrouded in gray, like my eager eyes,
When the wailing winds the blossoms blow through,
Like the hapless rhymes that I write to you?

Will you think of me when your wedding bell
Shall fall on my ear like a funeral knell,

To One Who Shall be Nameless.

When from me to another your steps depart,
And leave me alone with my aching heart?

Will you think of me on your wedding night,
While treading the aisle in your veil of white,
When the music swells and the soft lights shine,
And the bridal blooms in your tresses twine?

Will you think of me when you come at last
To regret your choice in the bitter past,
And know that I loved you far more than he,
When a great gulf severs your soul from me?

Then come back to me, my darling, my sweet,
With your gladsome face and your footsteps fleet,
With your springtime joys and your summer state,
Before we can say, "Too late, too late!"

HER SECRET.

AS I walked through the fields one day in June,
    When the world was warm with the richest
        of weather,
When the brooks and birds and bees where in tune,
    And Nature's whole heart was light as a feather,
I passed like a man in a blissful dream,
    Where the locust boughs with their clustered
        blooms
Seemed a palace of pearl or a cloud of cream,
    Or a peerless swan with the purest plumes.

And then from the sprays of the swinging flowers,
    A poor little bird dropped down at my feet,
As though a sharp lance had shot through the
        bowers,
    And taken the life of the songster sweet.
    She flitted and fluttered and ambled around,
She faltered and fled through the emerald grasses,
She flew through the air and fell on the ground,
    Down, down to the brook, with its reedy passes.

Said I "Little birdie, you can't fool me;
    For I know full well where your nest is swinging.
I know it is there in the locust tree,
    With the snowy clusters around it clinging.

But your nest and its pearls are safe, my dear,
   Be sure, little bird, I shall do you no wrong;
Return to your tree, sweet bird, never fear,
   And make your blithe nest bubble over with song."

And so when I see a little girl pout,
   And quarrel with him whom her heart loves best,
Desert him for others, run in and then out,
   I think of the bird who fled from her nest;
And I say, "Little girl, you can't fool me,
   For I am your sweetheart, my little white dove:
You can not deceive me, for at last I see,
   The priceless pearl of your precious love."

"EVERYTHING NEW UNDER THE SUN."

THE tone in which I speak to thee to-day
    Was never heard in all the years of yore;
My footstep falling as I reach thy door,
    Was never known through all the ages gray:
    My laughter, and my shudder of dismay,
Bear cadence never breathed on Earth before,
And having once been heard, shall nevermore
    Be heard or known, while ages pass away.

No lilac ever wore this same white wreath,
    No rose hath ever blushed with this same bloom,
And both are lost forever in a breath;
    I whisper soft, "I love thee," in the gloom,
In accents new, though old as life and death,
    That fade from earth forever in my tomb.

ORPHEUS AND THE SIRENS.

THE summer day waned over silent seas,
    Whose vast expanses stretched without a
        shore;
The skies extended like eternity,
And seemed to mingle with the boundless waves.
All day the weary mariners had gazed
To gain a prospect of some land, whose coves
Might be a haven for their sea-worn ship;
But still above and all around was naught
Save dreamy skies that hung o'er slumbering seas.
The evening slowly waned, the sun sank low
Above the waste of waters in the west;
And then behold! between them and the sun
A dark rock rose from out the briny waste;
Like to a towering cloud of night it seemed,
Where blent the sapphire sky and emerald sea.
Then Mopsus spoke, gray-haired Thessalian seer:
"Beware, beware! it is the Sirens' isle!"
So Jason cried, "Turn, turn the vessel's course!
Death waits us there; our life depends on flight.
Toil with your might, my oarsmen, for our hopes
Must now rely upon your sinewy arms."
The oarsmen strained their limbs with giant
        strength,
Their dark eyes glittered with a desperate hope,
Their brows were matted with a maze of frowns,

Their thews were twisted like an adder's coils.
But all for naught! some fearful fate had drawn
Their ship within the current gliding swift
Towards the jagged rock of certain death.
Then Orpheus spoke, the golden-throated king,
Whose strains were sweeter than harmonious
  spheres:
"Since might hath failed, my music now must win.
Oft have the warbling birds at dawn of day
Ceased all their notes to listen to my strains;
Oft have the woodland dryads stilled their songs,
Abashed before the sweetness of my lyre;
Apollo hearkens to the melody,
And merry Hermes pauses in his flight;
The growling leopard spares his trembling prey,
The bright-eyed eagle frees the fluttering dove;
Moved by those liquid notes, the hard rocks nod,
And leafy trees dance when the winds are still."

Lo! on the summit of the vaulting rock,
Behold the Siren with her golden hair!
See how the breezes wave the shining strands,
And clothe her bosom in a mellow maze!
Now see her soft arms clasp the magic lyre,
Her spotless neck bend o'er its silver strings,
Till, like the treasure of the swan's full nest,
It presses on her rounded, heaving breast.
And now the sun doth kiss the sky good-night,
Until her cheeks with burning blushes flame;
The brown crags flush amid the crimson glow,

The Sirens' fair forms bloom with ruby rays,
Like white-winged clouds at coming of the dawn
Enwreathed with roses plucked from heavenly
    bowers.

High on that rock the beauteous sisters stood,
Their lily fingers twined in tender clasp,
Their rounded shoulders touching, while their
    breasts
Heaved 'gainst each other in a sweet embrace;
Their soft bare feet gleamed like narcissus flowers.
But all the sailors shuddered when they saw
Pale, grinning skeletons strewn at those feet.
But soon their red mouths budded into song,
As blushing blossoms open in perfume;
So all the wide sea was entranced, and all
The sleeping waves awoke and laughed for joy.
The regal sun, enchanted in his course,
Stood still above the mighty world of waves,
And filled the darkest depths with ruddy light;
The sunburnt sailor's face was lit with love
And each dim eye flashed into starry flame.
Then from the Sirens' lips came melting tones,
Like honey-dew that drops from opening flowers:

AGLAIOPHEME.

"Come, bravest of heroes! I long and I yearn
    To fondle and fold you in blissful embrace,
To greet you with songs on your happy return,
    And cover with kisses each weary, worn face.

Long, long have I waited and watched for your sails,
  Still panting and pining with passionate sighs;
Desert the dark ocean, its rocks and its gales,
  And revel in glory of love-lighted eyes."

              THLEXIEPEA.

"Oh, come to me, lovers! repose on my heart!
  And swoon on Love's pillow and reel with his wine!
Come, waver no longer! we never shall part,
  Mine arms shall forever around you entwine;
My bosoms are budding like blossoming bowers,
  Where Love hath descended to build him a nest,
My kisses are sweeter than honey-gemmed flowers,
  And in my embraces are rapture and rest."

The liquid harmony filled all the air,
As mellow sunlight fills the summer sky;
The waves were babbling to the murmuring winds,
As lisping infants to their mothers' songs.
So all the mariners were mad with love,
And drunk with brightness of the Sirens' eyes;
They laughed and murmured with a maniac joy,
And sought to leap into the sea below,
So that they might at last find rest from toil,
And steep their senses in the wine of love.
But Orpheus stood unmoved, as if he scorned
To be enslaved by passion's fierce desire.
He sang and played, and lo! the sea-waves rose,
And dashed in playful joy about his feet;

The gray-winged sea-birds perched upon the mast,
The bright-hued dolphin waved his glittering tail,
The purple sea-weed rocked from side to side,
The blue-eyed naiads rose from coral bowers,
Their round cheeks gleaming through the emerald
    surge,
The black sea-snake uncurled his monstrous coils,
Made tame and harmless by his wondrous harp.
Oh, would that words had life, and verses souls,
To give a feeble image of his song!

ORPHEUS.

"Brave heroes! shall our honor dim with rust?
    Shall all our well-won laurels droop and fade?
Shall virtue's white star fall into the dust?
    Shall we retire to ignominious shade?
Fame's clarion voice calls to us in our shame,
    And sings of grander diadems to win;
What warrior here forgets his glorious name,
    And gives an ear to words of shame and sin?

"Awake! arise! death poisons all the air;
    Behold the ghastly skulls that strew yon shore!
New triumphs we should win, new dangers dare,
    And wondrous isles and trackless seas explore.
Think of the golden fleece our arms have won!
    Think of the mighty giants we have slain!
Away! our wondrous deeds are not yet done!
    Elysium's bowers our feet at last shall gain!"

AGLAIOPHEME.

"O heroes, with passion my dreams are afire,
   Enwreathing my fancies with flowers of flame;
My pulses are throbbing like strands of a lyre,
   And leaping with raptures no mortal can name.
Earth's maidens can never reward with such bliss;
   No frown of stern Pallas shall fetter my charms;
The mother who hushes her babe with a kiss
   Feels not the devotion which thrilleth mine arms."

THLEXIEPEA.

"Ye grasp at a shadow when seeking renown,
   And perish in battle enshrouded in blood;
But raptures and revels with Love shall flit down,
   And blessings and blisses his magic hath wooed.
O heroes, here endeth the tale of your toils,
   O wound not my spirit by turning away!
In pulses of passion forget your turmoils,
   And gather the roses while still it is May."

ORPHEUS.

"My comrades brave, list not unto their lays,
   The voice of death from lips of poisonous lust!
The paths of duty are the brightest ways,—
   Lift, lift your souls, thus groveling in the dust!
Our loved ones wait at home and watch in vain,
   Their fond eyes tearful in their lonely gloom;
Let us return and soothe their tender pain,
   Kissing their soft cheeks into brighter bloom.

"They wait beside the barren, restless sea,
   Their dark eyes dimmed with watching for our sail;
Shall we so heartless and perfidious be,
   As to forget their faces pure and pale?
How many eyes will sparkle when we come!
   How many hearts will bound with waking bliss!
Let us return unto our long-lost home,
   For only there hath earth its paradise."

His sweet tones died upon the raptured waves,
Which moaned and sighed to lose their balmy sounds,
And with the sun that faded out of sight
They left the lone sea desolate and dumb;
The dull blank silence that was left behind
Fell on the soul like stillness of the grave.
The songs had ceased, but Orpheus' harp had won,
That dreary night would be the Sirens' last!
The blithe breeze blew, and swelled the broad, white sails;
The hapless Sirens, weeping piteously,
Gazed with despair upon the fleeting ship
And bowed their heads beneath the shade of death.
Their golden hair fell drooping on their breasts,
Their rounded arms grew cold, their red cheeks paled;
Then rose their death-song, moaning deep and low,
Like some child's sob, so woful, tremulous,
Or, like the wail of chill November winds

Above the grave of summer's withered flowers,
And dying, dying, sinking, sinking low,
The Sirens' hearts were stilled, their eyes were
    dimmed;
The shades of night fell on the woful scene,
Their death-song fading in the gathering gloom.
  1886.

ETERNAL LOVE.

"For when they shall rise from the dead, they neither marry, nor are given in marriage; but are as the angels which are in heaven."—St. Mark xii. 25.

LOVE, they tell me mournful stories of the life beyond the tomb,
Whether spent in bowers of Eden or in lower worlds of gloom;
Thou art wise, dear love, my master, though the mortals call theé blind,
And I grope in tears and darkness; thou must now the pathway find.

Love, they tell me as I falter at the gate-way of the grave
Nevermore thy fond embraces nor thy kisses I shall crave,
Nevermere shall long to see thee, never long thy step to hear,
Though a thousand ages waiting, counting lingering year by year.

Love, they tell me in the caverns of the Charnel's realms of gloom
Never blush the sweet carnations nor the soft warm roses bloom;

And that solemn spirits treading in those mournful midnight bowers
Only see the chill camelias and the ghostly white moon-flowers.

Love, they tell me all are strangers on those dreary, dreary strands,
And each passes each in silence, smiling not nor grasping hands;
With those phantoms treading onward, passing still each other by,
Not a word of love is spoken, nor is heard a laugh or sigh.

Love, they tell me high-born ladies and the knights in armor there
Meeting in those dim recesses only gaze with chilly stare;
And that lovers and their loved ones, once so tender, warm, and true,
Never turn to look a moment, passing from each other's view.

Love, they tell me when those spirits shall at last ascend to heaven,
Wisdom, beauty, treasures, glory, all the gifts but love are given;
Though one spirit be in Eden, one in Hades' dumb despair,
This shall know the other's torment, yet will never shed a tear.

Love, I tell thee as I perish what my answer, love,
    shall be,
And my heart for both upwelling answers for thy-
    self and me—
Nearer, nearer, true love, nearer! gather fast the
    shades of night,
Kiss me, kiss me, dear love, kiss me! ere the fading
    of the light.

Though enrobed in funeral garments, I shall tear
    the shrouds away,
Breaking through the dismal charnel, walled with
    iron, stone, and clay,
Then with fingers torn and bleeding, pallid face,
    and bruiséd feet,
I shall wake thee in the midnight, stealing kisses
    warm and sweet.

Love, I tell thee, should they give me Paradise with
    all its bliss,
And I heard thee calling to me from the dark and
    dread abyss,
I would beg the demon porter to return thee to the
    light;
If he would not, I would join thee in thine anguish
    and thy night.

"JESUS WEPT."

MY Master bides not at the rich man's palace on this day,
Where mirth and music, wine and feasting speed the hours away;
His weary, way-worn feet have brought him to this lowly door,
And there the Prince of Heaven sits weeping with the friendless poor.

O blesséd Lord, friend of the friendless, happy should they be,
Their burning grief and anguish sharing side by side with thee!
For in this doubting age we can but moan and beg thy grace,
But can not see thy loving tears nor know thy gentle face.

Though in that rich man's palace swells the sound of revelry,
To-morrow in that palace shall the wail of anguish be;
Though in this poor man's hovel stalks the horrid spectre Death,
Soon shall He vanish at the great King's life-inspiring breath.

Oh, wondrous sight, a Monarch sitting in that humble cot!
Oh, wondrous sight, the Lord of angels with this hapless lot!
Oh, wondrous sight, here treads the ruler of the suns and stars!
Oh, wondrous sight, our God is weeping at Earth's prison bars!

I wonder if his moanings did not change to music sweet,
I wonder if the blossoms did not spring to kiss his feet.
I wonder if the watching angels gathered up those tears
And made them starry clusters, shining through the endless years.

For they were purer than the dews on lilies newly blown,
And lovelier than an empress' jeweled diadem they shone;
More radiant than the treasures that the sea's rich caves adorn,
More glorious than the Oriental splendors of the morn.

Those blesséd, blesséd tear-drops, falling on our dreary dearth,
Have wooed a golden harvest from the withered waste of earth,

Have melted, too, a myriad million selfish hearts of stone,
And blotted out uncounted sins in earth's vast records shown.

And though a thousand demons seek to give thy cause a thrust,
Those burning tears have worn their cruel daggers into rust!
And though a hundred empires at thee hurl their gathered powers,
Those holy tear-drops, like a flood, sweep down their haughty towers!

And though a host of bigots burning with a furious zeal
Have sought to aid their false creeds with the chain and stake and wheel,
Those tears have quenched their fires, torn down their mighty iron bars,
Thy cause triumphant still o'er steel and torch and wrecks and wars.

Oh, blesséd tears, with rainbow colors yearning earth illume!
Oh, blesséd tears, with lotus flowers make blissful heaven bloom!
Oh, blesséd tears, in mercy rain on all the spirits fell,
And like a mighty ocean quench the flaming gates of Hell!

THE GRAVEYARD.

ONCE I feared thee, mournful Monarch, with
    thy sad and solemn dells,
Haunted by the vesper shadows and the sobbing
    funeral bells;

Haunted by the ghostly roses, in their silken robes
    of white,
And the mock-bird's mystic singing in the dim and
    dusky night;

Haunted by the tombs of marble gleaming through
    magnolia leaves,
And the restless moonlight figures where the grave-
    mound dimly heaves.

But my loved ones gather with thee in the fading,
    fleeting years,
And I lay within thy caverns all my joys and hopes
    and fears.

Thou hast treasures in thy bosom richer than the
    ocean's caves,
Where the peerless pearls are beaming and the
    coral forest waves,

Where the mermaid gathers amber filled with
    mellow golden light,
And the silver-weighted galleons glimmer through
    the emerald night;

Thou hast hearts of gold within thee, hearts all
    priceless pearls above,
Rich with sweetness, rich with kindness, rich with
    never-dying love;

Thou hast dreams and aspirations sleeping with thy
    sheeted dead,
Wondrous visions, grand ambitions, from the earth
    forever fled.

Thou hast beauties in thy bosom blooming under-
    neath our feet,
Lovelier than our purple lilies and our jasmines soft
    and sweet;

Thou hast blue-eyed, dimpled children, with their
    mazy, golden hair,
Thou hast maids with brows of beauty, manly fig-
    ures sleeping there.

Thou hast wisdom in thy bosom greater than the
    lore of earth,
Gathered by its gray-haired sages from the dim
    creation's birth;

Thou hast infants in thy bosom, learned in secrets
    whispered low,
Which our wise men seek forever, never find, and
    can not know.

A VANISHED SUMMER.

THE dull December days, with garlands sere,
    Bear slowly, sadly on the dying year;
The somber hills, veiled in their mists of gray.
Like mourners in some haunted land away,
With haggard faces view the last sad hours
Of him whose spring-time wreathed their brows
        with flowers;
The wild north winds wail out a funeral hymn
Amid the bare boughs of the forests dim.

Soon will the chill storms scatter clouds of snow,
And stinging sleet and beating hailstones blow,
Like savage Cossack horsemen dashing by,
And fiercely clashing through the earth and sky;
While I, amid the desolation, yearn
For summer days that never can return,
Whose mellow skies and fragrant flowers have perished,
And now alone within my heart are cherished.

O gentle love, those happy hours are dead!
Our blissful summer has forever fled!
Yet often does my soul amid this rime
Crave and regret that long-lost happy time;
The frosty earth seems budding forth in flowers,
And liquid bird-songs fill the withered bowers,

A Vanished Summer.

The cold gray sky seems smiling down on me
When thinking of our summer by the sea.

How I remember now those golden days,
Robed in their dreamy, gleaming tropic haze!
The proud palmettos and the plumy pines,
The crimson roses and the trailing vines!
I see the green Savannah's leafy glooms,
Adorned by splendor of magnolia blooms,
The blushing oleanders, jasmines rare,
And mock-birds warbling in the ambient air!

How I remember now the sparkling sea,
Broad as the sky, grand as eternity!
How oft we sported with its playful spray,
Or watched the ships that glimmered far away!
We saw the mornings rise from garden bowers,
With pearly grottoes and with jeweled towers,
The evenings, with their ruby-clustered vines,
Exhaling clouds of misty, mellow wines!

We saw the white moon from the darkness bloom,
A water-lily in a lake of gloom!
Then through the twilight watched the timid stars,
Led by the crimson-crested hero Mars!
And then we told our old, old tale of love,
Until our spirits soared to skies above,
And guided by the splendor of thine eyes,
We trod with angels through that paradise.

Ah, summer garden, with the golden gate,
Thy blissful glories all are desolate;
Thy mellow sunshine now is lost in gloom,
Thy wondrous blossoms now are in their tomb;
Ah, summer ocean, with the playful waves,
Thy tropic splendors slumber in their graves!
Thy sweetest face is now forever banished,
Thy sweetest hope hath now forever vanished!

1885.

THE ONE LOVE.

THERE is a flower I long to call mine own,
    Most modest, frailest of the garden's blooms.
Within that bower the star-like lily looms,
The queenly rose reigns on her emerald throne,
The sweet carnation's breath is softly blown,
    The gorgeous tulip flames through leafy glooms.
    But love for that one flower my heart consumes;
My soul craves for her and for her alone.
The world hath other flowers of richer hue,
    And other buds will bloom when these have fled;
But with that flower doth pine my bosom true,
    And ne'er another love my soul shall wed;
My faded blossom can not youth renew;
    Nor life revive my one love that is dead.

"HE WHO HATH LOVED."

HE who hath loved hath borne a vassal's chain,
    And worn the royal purple of a king;
Hath shrunk beneath the icy Winter's sting,
Then reveled in the golden Summer's reign;
He hath within the dust and ashes lain,
    Then soared o'er mountains on an eagle's wing;
    A hut hath slept in, worn with wandering,
And hath been lord of castle-towers in Spain.

He who hath loved hath starved in beggar's cell,
    Then in Aladdin's jeweled chariot driven;
He hath with passion roamed a demon fell,
    And had an angel's raiment to him given;
His restless soul hath burned with flames of hell,
    And winged through ever-blooming fields of heaven.

UNSPOKEN LOVE.

I DARE not in thine ears my secret tell,
   And long in vain to say, "I love thee," sweet.
  False love is like a swallow, shrill and fleet,
True love a mock-bird, under some strange spell,
Who sings alone where midnight shadows dwell;
   One like a poppy, every face doth greet,
   While one, which never mortal eye shall meet,
Doth blossom like the fadeless asphodel.

False love speaks loudly, like a fickle wave,
   While, like the deep beneath the billow's roar,
True love doth hide its wondrous treasure-cave;
   One, like this life, is changeful, soon is o'er;
While one, like death, clasps in his silent grave,
   And keeps his secret, true forevermore.

"THOU LITTLE DREAMEST."

THOU little dreamest, as I gaze at thee,
    What visions gather in mine eager eyes;
Yet all the glory of the summer skies
Would vanish if thy face I could not see;
A dreary desert, where thou wert, to me
    A wondrous golden-city would arise;
    But all the earth, with myriad human ties,
A wilderness, without thee, sweet, would be.

For thee my heart shall, never ceasing, yearn
    Until my locks with winter snows are gray;
For thee its flame shall ever constant burn
    Until it flickers on my dying day;
To thee, my darling, it shall fondly turn
    Until it crumbles in the dust away.

SONNET.

ON MY TWENTY-FIRST BIRTHDAY, FEBRUARY 10, 1887.

THE restless years at last have reached this day,
   When youth must leave me, never to return,
   When Nature's kindly face grows cold and stern,
And life seems short, which once stretched far away.
No longer shall I rove through fields of May;
   New toils and cares are mine, hard truths to learn,
   Which ever faster fall from Sorrow's urn,
Since life no longer means a childish play.

O Voiceless Future! what fate dost thou hide?
   Hast thou a tale of darkness or of light?
Shall sin and sorrow snare my feet untried,
   And shall I stand or fall before their might?
But lose or win, or weal or woe betide,
   All is forgotten soon in endless night.

A BRIDAL BALLAD.

EARTH, enwreathed in emerald verdure, smiles in every dell and dale,
  Heaven, enthroned in regal splendor, bends with sparkling eyes above,
Morn arises with the glory of a wondrous fairy-tale,
  Night itself is bright with beauty, when the heart is filled with love.

Spring is tuneful with the trilling of a million merry birds,
  Queenly Summer's radiant blossoms flame in every field and grove,
Autumn, crowned with richest fruitage, laughs among his vines and herds,
  Even gruff and surly Winter smiles to see the face of love.

Youth, aglow with joys celestial, wreathes his golden locks with flowers,
  Age's path is strewn with garlands which a loving spirit wove,
Life reclines in regal beauty, singing under budding bowers,
  Even Death at last is conquered by the gentle hand of love.

But the earth is gray and wrinkled, heaven is draped in somber clouds,
  Morning's eyes are dim and tearful, twilight's shadows sadly rove,
All the year is dull and dismal, all its joys are in their shrouds,
  Life is but a funeral journey, to a heart bereft of love.

What is wealth, so hard and selfish, with its heaps of gems and gold?
  What is fame, so false and fickle, at whose words the masses move?
Wealth is but the icy grandeur of the Arctic mountains cold,
  Fame a fleeting desert phantom, when the soul has banished love.

But to-day, two souls united, never more to stray apart,
  Have begun their journey onward, all their plighted faith to prove;
Hope has robed the clouds with roses, joy is wreathing round each heart,
  Every step is strewn with lilies from the fairy-land of love,

And the days shall never darken, nor the pathway lead astray,
  While affection guides them onward like a gentle snow-white dove;

Youth shall flit in fadeless morning, all the months
    be merry May,
 Hope shall never be deceitful, while their hearts
    are true to love.

1888.

THE BYRON CENTENARY—1788-1888.

A HUNDRED summers since his first birthday
    Have shone in splendor, then have drooped
        and died ;
Earth's fond old heart has throbbed with joyous
        pride
To greet them with their garlands green and gay,
And ached with anguish as they passed away.
    But brightest summer decked her kingdoms
        wide
When unto Byron's lyre her mounts replied—
He perished, and her fields were sere and gray.

Her sweetest buds were blooming when he came,
    But fading as his footsteps turned to leave.
Among her sons is many a mighty name,
    But none like him, the reckless, bright, and
        brave.
He died, like music in a glorious dream,
    And Love's own heart was laid in Byron's grave.

A WEDDING SONG.

TWO roses nestling in one blissful bower,
    Two dew-drops in the bosom of a flower,
Two sweet birds singing songs of soft delight,
Two stars that meet in glittering fields of night,
Two roseate clouds that mingle far above,—
Such is the union of true hearts that love!

Our hopes are lovely in the morn of life,
But soon they perish in the harsh world's strife;
The sparkling wine-cup on the festal night
But sears the soul with baleful blast and blight.
Our dearest pleasures soon shall cease to move—
Earth hath no perfect joy save precious love.

With pearly treasures gathered from the sea,
Or starry gems from desert Araby,—
With golden heaps from India's wondrous caves,
Brought to their master by a thousand slaves,
The owner turns from that for which he strove
And feels but poor without some one to love.

As through chill mists around the wanderer's way
The sunshine steals to warm the dreary day;
As through the Winter night's enshrouding gloom
Soft Spring returns in all her maiden bloom;
So heaven comes like some pure white-winged dove
To bless the humblest cot where bides true love.

A Wedding Song.

May all your troubles be but April showers
To strew the way with rich and radiant flowers !
May angels hover with their outspread wings
To shield the nest where fond affection clings !
May blessings flit where'er your feet may rove,
And summer splendors wreathe the path of love !

THE FIRST TRANSGRESSION.

EVE, sweet tempter, lovely sinner, God hath cursed the deed which thou hast done,
Paradise is lost forever, and the stricken world's woes have begun.

Over Eden's eastern mountains flame the purple glories of the morn,
Welcomed by the waking warblers and the dewy blossoms newly born.

But I see the leaflets trembling, and I hear the quivering breezes sigh,
Feeling that for thy transgression thou and I and all the world must die.

Yet a spirit whispers to me that to save the world 'tis not too late,
If I turn my heart against thee, sin not, and desert thee to thy fate.

Then the fleeting years would scatter pallid autumn lilies on thy tomb,
I, thy consort, live forever, radiant with immortal youthful bloom.

Then mayhap the great Creator would another woman mould for me;
I might twine her locks with roses, give her kisses that I once gave thee.

The First Transgression.

But I could not, wondrous being! for thy smiles and
    wistful, pleading tears
Still would follow, hunt and haunt me through the
    maze of never-dying years.

Night's dim shades would find me ever lying by the
    bride I could not save,
And the piping birds at morning still would find me
    weeping at thy grave.

Earth would be a barren kingdom when, without
    my queen, to rest I stole,
Life eternal, bitter anguish, if I lost the idol of my
    soul.

Thou hast conquered, sweet enchantress! I forsake
    the fields of Paradise
For thy bosom's realm of rapture and the blissful
    glory of thine eyes.

It is done! I see the tiger, maddened, eyes ablaze,
    come creeping hither!
It is done! The birds cease singing, and our glori-
    ous garden bowers wither!

So my sons shall ruin empires, cast away their
    honor, treasures, fame,
Sink to hell and turn from heaven, when a woman
    bids them share her shame.

GLADSTONE.

1886.

Gathering snows of six-and-seventy winters
 whiten on thy lofty brow,
　Gathering glooms of six-and-seventy winters
　　hover round thy proud eye's fire,
And the mournful twilight hoary clouds thy lifetime's gentle sunset glow,
　While thy hopes, once so triumphant, in the
　　shadow of the tomb expire.

But above that waste of systems, strewn with ruins
　of the grand and great,
　Streams thy banner, still resplendent, as the
　　morning flames through dusky night,
Like a star thine eye still flashes, leading legions
　never to retreat,
　And thy form is still unbending, battling in the
　　burnished mail of Right.

Thou that scornest empty titles where the heart
　and soul are false and low,
　Thou that rendest chains of tyrants, forged in
　　feudal dungeons of the past,
Soon thine arms shall be victorious, soon thy hand
　shall deal a deadly blow,
　And the crowned oppressor's cohorts scatter as
　　before the autumn blast.

England's proudest kings are peasants placed beside
 thy peerless, princely mein,
 And their diadems are dimmer than the shadow
  of thy sunlike fame;
Thy crown jewels are the tear-drops of the grateful
 emerald ocean queen,
 And her never-fading garlands shall forever deck
  thy hallowed name.

Through the years shall live thy trophies, when thy
 soul hath rent its mortal bars,
 When Napoleon's arch of triumph in the gathering dust of time shall lie,
With a splendor never waning, like the wondrous
 never-dying stars,
 When the old earth's proudest empires like a
  morning mist have glimmered by.

DYNAMITE.

WELL may ye shudder at my name and curse my hour of birth,
Ye tyrants, hoarding misers, lords, and rulers of the earth!
For my hoarse voice will never soothe your ears with flattery,
But always bears unwelcome news unto the powers that be.

We can not love each other's ways, born under differing stars,
Ye under regal Hesper's beams, I under smouldering Mars;
Ye came into the world bedecked in silks and gems and gold,
I came in rags and tatters, wild with hunger and with cold.

I woke in stony dungeon cell, barred from the cheerful light,
Was fostered in the solemn shades of misery's tenfold night,
For golden chains were links of steel, for diamonds, tears of woe,
For rubies I had drops of blood brought by the tyrant's blow.

But I will heed no master's call, I never bend a
    knee,
Though despots seek to chain me down, I go forever
    free;
For in my sinews dwells the might of earthquake
    and of storm,
And jagged lightnings burst their bonds, hurled by
    my giant arm.

The massive feudal castles, knit with blocks of
    granite stone,
I heave on Titan shoulders till their turrets rock and
    groan,
The walls built in a hundred years fall as I lift my
    hand,
And palace towers by my breath are scattered like
    the sand.

And yet I bring with me a boon to weary human-
    kind,
And welcome is my awful arm to free heroic mind;
I tear the bolts from cells of woe and want and
    slavery,
In freezing mines, to lone exiles, I whisper "Thou
    art free!"

Ye princes of the earth, your dungeons shall restore
    their prey,
And bleak Siberia's dens shall feel the golden light
    of day.

Your gold can bribe me not, I fling your chains
 away to rust;
I sweep the earth with giant gales—remember ye
 are dust!
 1886.

SHELLEY.

1792–1892.

HE came amongst us, wandering from on high,
    Like golden-haired Apollo, long ago,
  To share with us our lives and labors low,
And gaze with longing on his native sky;
To sing sweet songs whose strains shall never die
    For weary mortals on their paths of woe;
    To cause a golden city's walls to grow
By magic of his heavenly harmony.

But now the singer hath forever flown,
    And left us beating still our prison bars;
His spirit over midnight's jeweled zone
    Returned to reign with Mercury and Mars
With Cassiopeia on her dazzling throne,
    And dusk Orion crowned with sparkling stars.

WILL HUBBARD KERNAN.

THOU art the poet of the realms of Night,
    Of anguish, desolation, and despair.
Like stern-browed Orcus leaping from his lair,
While Enna's blossoms withered in their fright,
Thou treadest through the earth with blast and blight,
    The sweet muse from her gardens glad to tear,
    That she thy mournful kingdom's gloom may shar
A bride enrobed in funeral garb of white.

She roams our fields when Spring is rich and green,
    And when the golden Summer crowns the years;
But when the Autumn's haggard face is seen,
    And icy Winter's stormy brow uprears,
Returns to be Death's sad and solemn queen,
    With thee, weird king of terrors and of tears.

A MODERN JULIET.

IF thou dost love me, and I love thee too,
   Wilt let them take thy sweetheart from thy side?
If I am for thee, who can be thy foe?
   If I am willing, wilt thou be denied?

Ah, laggard love, I pine in lonely halls,
   With hateful traitors thee and me between;
Wilt thou, my loyal subject, scale these walls,
   And liberate thy hapless captive queen?

'Tis true no swords or spears surround my court,
   But worldly craft is now the sentinel;
'Tis true I'm guarded not by fleet and fort,
   But Wealth and Avarice watch my prison cell.

Yet in that fortress thou hast friendly hands,
   Two little rebels, who will steal its key,
With potions lull to sleep the sentry bands,
   And then betray the castle unto thee.

Oh, fear no foe; naught can withstand thy powers
   When thou dost love, and I thy love return;
To steal a kiss Love breaks through stony towers,
   And Love to win Love laughs the world to scorn.

He loves not who hath not the heart to dare
    The woman that he loves from foes to take;
She loves not who will not his portion share,
    Though forced to give the whole world for his sake.

Wilt raise the siege, and bid thy hosts depart,
    When I'd surrender if thou shouldst command?
When God hath given unto thee my heart,
    Wilt let a mortal rob thee of my hand?

Then take the kiss I long to give to thee,
    And spite the scheming, envious world outside;
I all in all to thee, and thou to me,
    With Love our world, a kingdom rich and wide.

THE PRINCE'S WEDDING.

I AM standing here forsaken in my lonely attic room,
Hair disheveled, lips contorted, fierce eyes glaring in the gloom.

In the streets I hear the shouting of the gay and giddy throng,
Mad with mirth and mad with music, sweeping like a flood along;

Streaming under silken banners, under leafy arches green,
Strewing roses in the pathway of the nation's future queen;

Here they come in festal raiment, eyes aglow and faces bright!
Mounted guards with gilded trappings, beauteous maids bedecked in white!

Here they come, the little children, in their holiday attire!
Here they come, the bands of music, setting every heart afire!

But my bosom aches with anguish, and I long in
    vain to die,
As my startled babe awakens with a painful, piteous
    cry.

Ah, my babe, my helpless outcast! now my shame,
    though once my joy,
Pierce me not with fiercer tortures; hush thee, hush
    thee, pretty boy!

Thou shouldst be a prince, my darling, robed in
    silken garments soft,
Not in lowly rags and tatters in this squalid attic
    loft;

I should be a queen, my darling, wreathed with
    dazzling diadems,
On a golden throne reclining, jeweled o'er with
    starry gems.

For the prince, boy, is thy father, thou and I should
    share his name,
But the traitor now hath spurned us, hurling us to
    scorn and shame.

Now the city shouts his praises on his merry wed-
    ding-day,
While the woman he hath ruined crouches trembling
    in his way!

Man may dye his brow with crimson, yet may wear a lily wreath,
And may hide his hateful treason like a dagger in its sheath;

Woman, having once worn scarlet, nevermore shall wear the white
Till the pallid shroud enfolds her in the charnel's cheerless night.

See the nuptial's grand procession, marching proudly in the sun,
Heedless of thy wailing mother with her shame and sin undone!

See the beauteous bride my darling! She who stole thy father's love!
See her, robed in spotless garments, like a peerless, snow-white dove!

See my loved one there beside her! See his eyes with rapture fill!
O my prince, my lord, my master, how I love thee, love thee still!

How I crave one look of pity, how I crave one farewell sweet!
How I long to cry unto thee, how I long to kiss thy feet!

O my prince, my God, remember, thou didst once
    my love return,—
But thou wilt not hear or heed me as with mad-
    dened heart I yearn.

Hark, the wedding bells are pealing! She is
    stealing him from *me!*
Curses on thee, happy maiden, how I envy, envy
    thee!

Hark, the wedding-bells ring faster! I am thrilled
    with madness dire!
Hark, the throbbing peals grow louder! Heart
    and soul are all afire!

I am furious, frantic, frenzied, as I clutch my
    dagger's hilt;
I am coming, coming, coming! Tremble, tremble
    in thy guilt!

Now I hurl my wailing infant in thy rearing horse's
    path!
Now my dagger in thy bosom quenches swift it's
    flaming wrath!

It is done! My babe lies mangled underneath the
    horse's feet!
It is done! Thou liest bleeding, dying in my arms,
    my sweet!

* * * * * * *

Now I hear the hammers ringing as the gallows rises there;
They have tied my hands behind me, they have shorn my waving hair.

Now I see the noose adjusted, as they bring the sable hood;
Now I see the rabble gather, as they clamor for my blood.

But, my prince, I still have conquered, thou art mine for evermore!
Thou canst not, my sweet, evade me, I shall leave thee nevermore!

Though thy soul should soar to heaven, and should pass the pearly gate,
And the angels should surround thee, in thy splendor and thy state,

I would knock upon those portals, like a ghost from haunted lands,
And thy heart should quake with terror at those beating, bony hands.

I would come with funeral garments as beneath the gallows drest,
I would show my murdered infant, bleeding on my pulseless breast,

Glazéd eyes from sockets starting, lips protruding,
    they should see,
And my neck with blue rings circled, where the
    hangman strangled me.

From thy kindly Saviour's bosom I thy shuddering
    soul would tear,
And mine arms should clasp around thee, dragging
    thee to Hell's despair,

Through the wilds below to wander, lost to light
    and lost to hope,
Thou and I bound fast forever by the hangman's
    hempen rope.

Though the servile world hath crowned thee, thou
    at last shalt share my shame;
Though the worldly priests absolve thee, thou shalt
    share my couch of flame.

ELIZABETH AND ESSEX.

FORGIVE thee, writhing, gasping viper, doomed,
    despairing soul?
Forgive thee, heartless traitor, who from me my
    Essex stole?
I tell thee, dying woman, as the death-dews gather
    chill,
I loathe thy face—God may forgive thee, but I
    never will.

The weary, weary years that part me from my
    Essex' side
Have vanished, and I live again the hapless day he
    died;
The dead Past rises with its ghastly visage from the
    tomb,
As on that awful morning when my Essex met his
    doom.

I see the scaffold looming dimly on that dreadful
    day,
To which my darling Essex soon must wend his
    woeful way;
I see the headsman standing masked in black and
    draped in red,
With cruel steel axe gleaming, hungry for my
    Essex' head.

His locks which oft I fondled soon must roll into dust,
His soft cheeks whiten at the sharpened axe's ponderous thrust,
The lips I kissed so often soon be bleeding, chill and stark,
His bright eyes, that I worshipped, soon be closed and dim and dark.

O Essex, Essex! I am waiting, longing to forgive!
O Essex, Essex! stifle struggling pride, consent to live!
O Essex, Essex! hearken, let not Death come in between!
O Essex, Essex! hear, oh, hear thy true love and thy queen!

Alas! he hears not, and he will not send me back the ring,
Whose golden circlet would have made the fettered captive king.
And now my heart is withered, life is choked with agony,
For Essex treads the scaffold, there to bow his head and die.

Since then the birds of Spring-time sing in vain to soothe my woe,
Since then the Summer blossoms lighten not my footsteps slow,

Since then the winds of Autumn taunt me with his
    dying wail,
Since then the snows of Winter haunt me with his
    visage pale.

A thousand blushing maidens in my realms stroll
    forth to-day
To meet fond lovers who will woo them on their
    happy way,
While I, their queen becrowned, bejeweled, wildly
    wring my hands,
For my true lover wandering in the cheerless spirit
    lands!

Can I forgive thee, who didst hide from me the
    fatal ring?
Can I forgive thee, traitor to my love, my lord, my
    king?
No, I will curse thee as thou diest, like a demon
    fell,
And when I follow I will hound thee through the
    fields of hell.

Forgive thee, writhing, gasping viper, doomed, de-
    spairing soul?
Forgive thee, heartless traitor, who from me my
    Essex stole?
I tell thee, dying woman, as the death-dews gather
    chill,
I loathe thy face—God may forgive thee, but I
    never will.

MY QUEEN.

THERE is but one maid whom my soul doth love,
  And she is sweeter than a budding flower.
  She standeth in a haughty castle tower,
And sees me, burdened vassal, from above;
Through marble halls of wealth her footsteps move,
  While want and famine round my rude hut lower;
  She reigneth in a wondrous royal bower,
While I, an outcast, on the highway rove.

But oft beneath the mellow, mazy moon
  I sing her love-songs till the morning light;
Oft steal we through the blooming fields of June,
  And there, in secret, lovers' pledges plight;
Sweet Poesie! the splendor of my noon,
  My rose of morning, and my star of night.

WHEN I GET RICH.

"WHEN I get rich, when I get rich," I
whisper to my heart,
"O'er scattered roses thou shalt on thy march of
triumph start,
Thy golden visions evermore shall fold their fickle
wings,
And lead me, robed in purple, through the halls of
queens and kings.

"As some wan, wasted flower, beneath the parching desert skies,
Hath fainted with the fervor till the rain-drops ope
its eyes,
And as in tearful dreams one sees a sweet face long
denied,
And starts, awakens, finds the loved one sitting by
his side,

"So thou, poor, weak, discouraged heart, with
wistful waiting sore,
Shalt waken, and thy yearning shall be soothed for
evermore;
For I shall conquer Fortune, heartless, ever-change-
ful witch,
Thy hopes shall all be granted when thy master
shall be rich!"

But this I've whispered vainly to my heart a thousand times
In youthful years long perished and through age's curfew chimes,
As some fond mother, kissing back the sobs and childish tears,
With wondrous fairy-stories lulls her little loved one's fears.

"My castle turrets shall arise above a craggy height,
Around them in the heavens kingly eagles wing their flight,
With winding rivers, lakes, and fields, and forests far below,
Their ancient summits blooming in the morning's crimson glow."

But now my castle crumbles, through its halls the ravens wing,
Around its ruined columns mournful ivy tendrils cling;
I see its haggard turrets gleam like spectres of the night,
I see its ghastly windows blindly stare at morning's light.

"When I have treasures I shall win for thee thy maiden sweet,
And thou, poor heart, discouraged! shalt not wither at her feet;

With wreaths of starry diamonds I shall deck her
    golden hair,
Her beauty shall surrender, she shall save thee
    from despair!"

Ah me! my poor heart waited vainly for that happy
    day,
A richer lover won her, bore the maiden far away;
Another's are the kisses that I loved to think were
    mine,
Another's fingers fondly in her locks those circlets
    twine.

"My sword shall conquer empires, and my sceptre
    awe the earth,
My kingdom grandest, broadest, since the gray
    creation's birth,
My wisdom rise triumphant o'er the secret of the
    tomb,
My fame still thunder onward till the judgment
    dawn of doom."

Alas! mine eyes were lustrous, but their morning
    splendor dies,
Youth's feet are winged like eagles, and away he
    fleetly flies;
So now I falter feebly with the bleeding, dying
    day,
My promise still is broken, and my locks are
    growing gray!

"When I get rich, when I get rich!" Poor heart, believe it not!
I'll keep one promise only: thou shalt share the common lot;
Beside thy dead dreams lying, in some charnel's dusty niche,
At last thou'lt slumber equal to the haughty and the rich.

THE POSTMAN.

POSTMAN, postman, what hast thou for me?
    Shall there never end to waiting be?
Postman, postman, hast the letter there
Giving me to rapture or despair?

Bearing letters full of golden light,
Bearing letters full of mournful night,
Bearing letters full of Summer bloom,
Bearing letters full of Winter gloom!

Bearing letters full of hope and cheer,
Bearing letters full of doubt and fear,
Bearing letters like a gathered sheaf,
Garnered gladness, thorns and tares of grief!

Thou dost bring to grasping misers old,
Gleaming heaps of silver and of gold,
Thou dost tell the broken merchant's heart
News of loss and panic on the mart.

In some attic, to a humble door,
Where doth dwell some striving soul obscure,—
Struggling genius with an unknown name,—
Thou dost bring a poet's regal fame.

In some palace to a sceptred king,
Thou dost desolating tidings bring,

And he trembles, hearing thee repeat
News of wreck and ruin and defeat.

Thou dost all the prisoner's woe dispel,
Bringing news of pardon to his cell,
Thou dost stab a mother's bounding joy,
Bringing farewells from her dying boy.

Postman, postman, here in doubt I rove!
Bring me kisses from the maid I love.
Bid her light the darkness of despair
With a ringlet from her golden hair!

BYRON.

His heart was moulded in the weakness of the crumbling dust and clay,
Yet mighty as the summit of some giant granite mountain gray;

His fancy twined the blushing roses round the crystal cup of mirth,
Then like a fleeting phantom wandered through the desert's parching dearth;

Within his portals Love was throned in richest Oriental state,
While at his doorway crouched the thistles and the loathsome weeds of hate;

His spirit knew not Spring-time's songsters, nor her dewy, waking flowers,
But loved the sad magnificence of Autumn's gorgeous dying bowers;

His feet were strangers to the purple morning's palaces of light,
But haunted vistas where the twilight's tearful eyes grew dim with night.

The world hath grander, purer bards, like Alps enthroned on spotless snow,
While he, like raging Ætna, flames forever with a fevered glow;

But round their chilly crowns of ice the timid blossoms fear to twine,
Whilst 'midst his lavas spring the olive and the purple-clustered vine.

The world hath poets who from tears and thraldom rose to royal fame,
While he from state descended to assume the bard's and patriot's name;

They with the spell of old Timotheus raised their muses to the sky,
While he, like Saint Cecilia, drew his seraph earthward from on high;

His name, though pierced by despot's dagger and the envious bigot's thrust,
Shall live when Europe's tongues are silenced and the lips that spake them dust.

TO DR. J. J. WHEAT.

THERE is a wondrous power in earthly song,
   Whose eagle spirit soars to Paradise,
Too free and happy for this world of wrong,
   Too grand and glorious for our clouded skies.
The liquid bird-notes at the dawn of day,
   The laughing winds that kiss the budding flowers,
Breathe echoes of an Eden far away,
   And sing the beauties of its fadeless bowers.
Our yearning hearts leap forth with them to soar,
   And by their airy wings are borne on high;
We break the chains of clay which once we wore,
   And feel too happy for a tear or sigh.

But eloquence like thine can sway the mind
   More strongly than the trumpet's loftiest peal,
More deeply than the moaning midnight wind,
   More sweetly than the witching wavelet's spell.
The organ's grand triumphant harmony
   Moves not the soul more than thy swelling voice,
The master-singer's notes that mount on high
   Have not more power to make man's heart re-rejoice.
And like Arion singing to the sea,
   Till gathering dolphins shone like rainbow clouds,
I marvel as thou bringest forth for me
   Sweet dreams and visions out of tombs and shrouds.

To Dr. J. J. Wheat.

When listening to thee, Fancy breaks her bars,
   And follows in thy free, unbounded flight;
She wends her way beyond the farthest stars,
   And bathes her pinions in eternal light.
We wander with thee by blue Galilee,
   Where every wavelet sings a sacred song;
The vine-clad rocks of Nazareth we see,
   Where Jesus, weak and foot-sore, passed along.
We see poor Mary shedding bitter tears,
   Which wash forever all her sins away,
And then the woman at the well, who hears
   Of that unfailing fount which springs in endless day.

A VISION IN ASHES.

THE flames flicker low on the shadowed hearth,
    The cricket's quaint carol is faintly ringing;
My heart, like the flames as they leap from earth,
    Through vistas in dream-land is swiftly winging.
I think of the hours in the spectral past,
    Whose echoes are softly and sadly sighing;
Once more through the vales of that elf-land vast
    I wander through bowers, now dead or dying.

I think of my youth, with its eager eyes,
    Its royal romances forevermore vanished;
I think of my hopes, with their morning skies,
    Whose fancies have faded, whose blossoms are banished;
I think of my castles, now sunk in decay,
    Uprearing gaunt ruins through dead years dreary;
Of golden-haired joys that are now grown gray;
    Of visions departed and dreams grown weary.

I think of the friends who are friends no more,
    All turning their fancies to newer faces;
While I, left alone with a heart so sore,
    Must wander dejected through stranger places.
I sigh as I think of the true ones dead,
    I fancy their pinions still flit around me;
Of dead golden days,—they are now like lead,—
    Ah, meshes enchanted, ye still surround me!

I sigh for the spring that can not return,
    Whose roses are withered, whose sweet birds scattered;
In vain for the summer now lost I yearn,
    Whose bowers are yellow, whose green leaves shattered;
I look over earth that is gaunt and gray,
Where autumn's chill showers and blasts are flying,
    And then through the skies of the fading day,—
All nature doth hearken and answer sighing!

And such is our life, with its sparkling morn,
    With visions that perish, with idle dreaming,
With hopes that desert us when weary and worn,
    And sunset is faintly and coldly gleaming.
The embers grow pale, lose their youthful fire,
    And ashes all sombre fall over their glory.
So thus all my dreams and my hopes expire,
    And no one will heed them or hear their story.

A FIRESIDE PHANTOM.

AH, have pity, silent spectre, with thy sad, reproachful gaze,
  Haunting still my shadowed hearth-stone in the twilight dim and drear;
For, my darling, we can never call to life our perished days,
  And forever separated are the souls once near and dear.

Once we roved the fields together, hand in hand, with thoughtless joy,
  When thy lips were sweet with laughter and thine eyes unstained with tears,
Thou a little fair-haired maiden, I a fond and dreaming boy,
  Ere we tasted worldly sorrow in these hapless later years.

Oh, how green those leafy woodlands! Oh, how blue those summer skies!
  Oh, how wild the thrush's warblings! Oh, how clear the bubbling springs!
Oh, how sweet the vine's dark clusters! Oh, how rich the rose's dyes!
  Earth was strewn with budding garlands, heaven was white with angel wings!

Then thy dark-blue eyes would charm me with a
    blithesome, blissful spell,
  And thy soft cheeks' darling dimples bound me
    like a chain of flowers;
Then thy ringing laugh would thrill me,—ah, I
    hear its echo still!
  And thy silver songs were sweeter than the birds'
    in woodland bowers.

Hand in hand we wandered ever, viewing many a
    wondrous land,
  Eastern realms whose sands were golden,
    diamond valleys, pearly caves,
Fairy isles and haunted mountains, dream-land's
    weird enchanted strand,
  Knights and maids in grim old castles, treasures
    sunk beneath the waves.

But, alas! those dreams have vanished, all those
    days forever fled,
  Life no longer is a poem, but a lesson dull and
    dry;
Youth, grown sere and gray and faded, in the lap of
    age lies dead,
  Summer's golden-hearted blossoms sleep where
    winter's chill winds sigh.

Cruel want hath spurred me onward, toiling for a
    loaf of bread;
  Hateful avarice chilled my bosom, struggling for
    the gleam of gold.

So, sweet Poesie, I left thee, though my soul to thee was wed,
Though I loved thee, seraph maiden, more than mortal tongue hath told.

Like the foolish shepherd Paris, I was doomed to make a choice,
Whether I should take thy rival or should still around thee cling.
"Oh, choose me, who love so fondly!" came thy gentle, pleading voice.
"I will make of thee a poet who is greater than a king!

"I shall cling to thee forever, thou shalt be my prince, my pride,
Green and never-fading laurels round thy brow my hand shall twine;
Though thy path be dark and dismal, I shall not desert thy side,
Thine shall be my bliss and beauty and thy sorrows shall be mine."

"But," thy rival quickly answered, "she will make thee poor and low,
Press thee down to scoffs and sorrows, doom thy life to shame and scorn;
Yet, if thou wilt but desert her, fame and fortune I'll bestow,
And for earth's enchanting splendors thou shalt never vainly yearn.

"All her gifts are false and empty, all her promises are vain,
    And her laurel wreaths are only strewn upon her victim's tomb;
Then, desert her! I will give thee pleasures unalloyed with pain,
    In the present, not the future, after life hath met its doom."

Then my treacherous heart disowned thee, and I grasped thy rival's prize,
    Left thee weeping, left thee lonely, like a poor forsaken child.
Ah! again I see thee, darling, with thy mournful tear-stained eyes,
    With thy golden locks dishevelled and thy sweet face wan and wild.

Then too late I called upon thee to return unto mine arms,
    For thy happy heart was broken and thy olden gladness fled.
Nevermore upon my bosom I shall press thy sweet young charms,—
    All in vain I kissed thy dimples, thou wert cold and still and dead!

Still thy gentle spirit haunts me, as the pensive twilight falls,
    And thy dear blue eyes gaze on me by my shadowed, lonely hearth;

Round my neck thy soft arms gather, and thy kind voice sweetly calls,
So I dread thy shade no longer, stealing back to share my dearth.

TRIUMPHANT LOVE.

TO love and be loved! I tremble with joy,
    'And fancy is blooming in splendor and glory;
To love and be loved! I dream like a boy
    Who wanders through gardens of romance and
        story.

For love is a gem that lights a dark mine,
    As islet of verdure that decks a gray ocean,
A fount in the waste, of sweetness divine,
    A rainbow allaying the storm's wild emotion.

'Tis love that gives life one chalice of bliss,
    And strews the grave's gateway with garlands
        of flowers;
Like spring, it awakes the years with a kiss,
    And wreathes the earth's thistles with blossom-
        ing bowers.

The peasant who's loved is rich as a king,
    The king who is hated is poorest of mortals;
Sweet love to lost souls bright blessings may bring,
    And banished, leave darkened high heaven's
        pearl portals.

The soul without love! A bird that ne'er sings,
   A palace deserted to silence and sadness!
The soul without love! A god without wings,
   An Eden whose angels have never known gladness!

To love and be loved! the rest is all dross,
   For fortune and fame are heartless and sterile,
They canker with rust or mantle with moss,
   Their glory is shrouded in funeral apparel!

A throne and a crown are rigid and cold,
   The eye of the serpent gleams forth from each jewel,
While love doth gild huts with riches untold,
   And warm into mercy the hearts of the cruel.

I loved and am loved! what more can life give?
   Thy bosom, O darling, I clasp and I cherish;
Thy kisses would cause the dead to revive,
   Or lead me, O precious, to wither and perish!

Come go with me, sweet! thy breast I enfold,
   Let passion's wine chalice enchant us forever!
Our romance and love shall never grow cold,
   And we shall be severed, my sweetest one, never!

Through life we shall pass with hand clasped in hand,
   And shrouded in cerements, still fondly be clasping,
Together to tread on Eden's bright strand,
   Or wander unsevered where wild fiends are gasping!
1888.

THE OLD COLLEGE DAYS.

(Written for and read before the Seventeenth Biennial Convention of the Sigma Chi Fraternity, Chicago, August 31, 1888.)

THE hours that have fled seem blithest and best,
    The days that are dead most blissful and bright,
The sweetest on earth were lips we then pressed,
    The warmest were hearts now silenced in night.
The locks we caressed were fullest of splendor,
    The tones that we heard the softest e'er spoken,
The faces we loved most true and most tender,
    Those flowers most fair whose bowers are broken.

The hearts that now beat may charm and delight,
    But those that are still were kindest of all;
Sweet voices may still to pleasure invite,
    But not as the tones we can not recall.
The eyes that still wake our souls to devotion
    Are never so bright as those that have vanished,
The lips we still touch may thrill with emotion,
    But never like those now silenced and banished.

The old college days were gayest e'er known,
    The old college friends the truest on earth,
The love of those friends the surest e'er won,
    The souls of those friends the fullest of mirth.

The boys we then loved were braver and brighter,
   Their faces the frankest e'er gathered together,
The throb of their hearts was quicker and lighter,—
   Ah me! the whole year was soft summer weather.

But now the fleet years grow gloomy and chill,
   The light of the skies is mantled in clouds,
The voice of our mirth grows saddened, then still,
   The raptures of yore are laid in their shrouds;
The dear college friends are scattered asunder,
   The dear college boys tread scenes full of sorrow,
Alone and in doubt the wide world we wander,
   And lose the bright past in each dark to-morrow.

Still, oft in these days of darkness and doubt,
   When life from its height begins to decline,
Amid the dim shades a star will shine out,
   Sweet birds sing their songs and fair flowers twine.
For out the dead past sweet voices come ringing,
   Perfumes of dead flowers revive and flit hither,
Bright faces we knew like angels come winging,
   When old college friends again meet together!

And now on this night we gather in mirth,
   Like shades of old Danes in Odin's feast-hall,
And talk of old friends, the fullest of worth,
   And talk of old times, the dearest of all.
Like sailors long tossed on billows of ocean,
   We'll rest us at last with songs and with stories;
Like soldiers long driven by war's wild commotion,
   Reposing, we boast our trophies and glories.

Then, comrades, fill up each goblet with wine,
  Till bubbles and beads peep over the brim,
Then lift them on high, like rubies to shine,
  Or flaming red stars when twilight grows dim;
Now drink to the days deserted forever,
  And drink to the joys that now have departed;
Now drink to the souls that fate can not sever,
  And drink to the dead, so brave and true-hearted.

May life for us all strew dreams full of joy,
  And bring every hope to flower and fruit!
May each have the heart and soul of a boy,
  Where age's cold craft forever is mute!
May all tread the earth with hand in hand twining,
    Through meadows bedecked in brightest of blossom,
And passing away, all free from repining,
  Recline in one bower in Eden's soft bosom!

THE MOCKING-BIRD.

(FROM AN INDIAN LEGEND.)

I.

I GAZED at a mock-bird high in a tree,
   And this was the song he warbled to me:

II.

THOU wond'rest why, as aloft I soar,
I sing to thee not the same strains o'er,
And marvel much that the notes I pour
By other blithe birds were trilled before,
And every sound on the sea or shore
I mimic and mock for evermore.

III.

FAR beyond the mystic mountains,
   Far beyond the sunset's throne,
Where the crystal western fountains
   Bubble through the forests lone,

Lived an Indian tribe now perished,
   I their prince in days of old;
Yet a maiden sweet I cherished
   In a neighboring nation's fold.

But our tribes were foemen ever,
    So our love we dared not tell,
And I saw her sweet face never
    Till the twilight shadows fell.

Then with stealthy steps I sought her
    With a signal sharp and shrill,
Till the foeman chieftain's daughter
    Joined me in the woodland still.

I would mock the thrush in flying,
    Or the katydid at night,
Hooting owl or panther crying,
    So her steps were guided right.

Then we two would roam together,
    Kissing in the friendly gloom,
Till the blooming stars would wither
    And the night sink in her tomb.

But together once they found us,
    And they doomed us both to die;
To the stake they dragged and bound us,
    Where the cruel flames streamed high.

But the great God heard our sighing:
    In the sky a storm upreared;
From the smoke two birds came flying,
    And the lovers disappeared.

Yet we heedless twain had ever
   Gazed but in each other's eyes,
Impious souls, had worshipped never
   Him who rules within the skies.

So he saved us but to doom us
   Through the moons to roam apart,
While despair shall e'er consume us,
   Reigning o'er each breaking heart.

I, a mock-bird, fondly singing,
   Robed in sombre ashen gray,
She, with gorgeous plumage, winging
   In some forest far away.

IV.

My tongue must twitter through all the hours,
Still mocking each sound in woodland bowers,
The wail of winds and the sobs of showers,
The cricket's shrill chirp in fading flowers,
The night-hawk's cry in her pine-tree towers,
The bark of the wolf when midnight lowers.

But then at last, in a dim, sweet year,
When gray with despair and gray with fear
And mocking still at the sounds I hear,
I'll trill the true note that strikes mine ear,
The song that's sung by my long-lost dear,
And then her sweet face shall reappear.

Till then this song over forests wide
I sing as I seek my banished bride:

V.

I am seeking for thee ever through the emerald
    woods of May,
I am seeking for thee ever through October's
    fields of gray;

I am seeking for thee ever through the June-time's
    golden glory,
I am seeking for thee ever through December's
    twilight hoary;

I am seeking for thee ever where the morning
    buds are blooming,
I am seeking for thee ever where the vesper shades
    are looming;

I am seeking for thee ever through the dazzling
    tropic noons,
I am seeking for thee ever under wan and wasted
    moons;

I am striving still to find thee through the green
    magnolia-trees,
I am striving still to find thee by the misty north-
    ern seas;

I am striving still to find thee in the palmy Indian
    islands,
I am striving still to find thee in the chill and track-
    less highlands;

I am striving still to find thee on the crimson cactus-blossoms,
I am striving still to find thee in the white lake-lilies' bosoms;

I am striving still to find thee in the realm of Aztec mild,
I am striving still to find thee in the land of Huron wild.

So I seek thee always faithful, seek thee, sweetest, thus forever,
But I find thee in my roamings banished, vanished darling, never!

VI.

Hear the blackbird, silver-throated, calling me to meet him in the breezy boughs,
Hear the jay, so blithe and buoyant, bidding me to join him in his mad carouse;

Hear the redbird, wild and wilful, teasing me to aid him in some curious quest,
Hear the bluebird, sweet and soothing, bidding me to come and see his happy nest;

Hear, amid pink-blossomed orchards, wooing, cooing of the fond enamoured dove,
And the oriole, her rival, begging me to bless her with my love.

But my heart is ever faithful; never shall another
    love be known to me;
Though the myriad ages wither, in my visions only
    one sweet face I see.

VII.

I burn,
I long, I yearn,
Through chilly autumns red,
Where blasted, burning deserts spread,
To see thy gentle, tender, loving face,
And hear once more thy wild, sweet, fawn-like
    tread of grace!

I've not
Thy love forgot;
Then wilt thou let me pine
Far from thy starry eyes divine?
Return, return! then like a merry boy
I'll sing forever for thee thrilling tunes of joy!

VIII.

Indian wigwams, Indian camp-fires from their ruth-
    less pale-faced foes have vanished,
And the red-men, like the red leaves, on a hoary
    winter blast are banished.

All our sacred groves have fallen, all the trophies
    of our tribe have perished,
All our legends long forgotten, and our mother-
    tongue no longer cherished.

But amid the desolation, ever vainly for thy presence pining,
Never in my tearful visions have I seen thy glorious plumage shining.

Yet another love can never make me drink from out his bubbling chalice,
And no other maiden woo me to abide within her blissful palace.

I shall love thee till the spring-time thrilleth not the earth's breast with emotion,
I shall love thee till the dew-drops all have vanished from the desert ocean.

Though I find thee, beauteous being, not till all the mountains burst asunder,
And the judgment trumpet rouses all the earth's dead like a peal of thunder.

"YE BACHELOR."

OLD friend, you ask me why, on this November night,
When every home is filled with life and love and light,
I sit here lonely in this desolated room,
Beside this dying fire, and in this gathering gloom?

Yes, it is glorious on this gay Thanksgiving Night,
To look into those homes, so blithesome and so bright,
And sweet to see the loving eyes, the faces fair,
To hear the pattering feet of little children there.

Yes it is true, I often wish to steal away
From out the shadows of these dismal walls of gray,
But as I light my pipe, its smoke-wreaths pinions take,
And gazing in that smoke a thousand dreams awake.

So I am not alone, although you smile at me,
And in this dingy place no friendly face you see;
For in the darkness beckon airy spirit hands,
And wandering with them I am borne to wondrous lands.

And now I see a dell with overhanging bowers,
Bedecked in sunshine and a wealth of summer flowers.

I hear the bubbling brook, I hear the lowing herds,
I hear the singing of a thousand blissful birds.

And in the leafy lanes I see a little face,
Upon whose cheek no sin or sorrow shows a trace;
Fresh as a blossom jeweled with the dews of morn,
Pure as a young dove in the leafy branches born!

Her eyes are darker than the purple pansies there,
Her laughter lighter than the bird-songs in the air;
Her cheeks are softer than the peach-tree's clustering bloom,
Her lips are sweeter than the lilac's frail perfume.

And there we tread in joy, with golden skies above,
With humming bees, and birds that carol lays of love.
Her golden hair has snared me in a maze of bliss;
Earth fades and heaven descends around us as we kiss.

Another vision comes: I see her lying still,
With snowy blossoms in her waxen fingers chill.
Her sweet, pale little face, that never knew a cloud,
Is mantled round with silken foldings of the shroud.

Another vision still: I see a new-made grave,
Above whose clods November's wild winds madly rave,

With snow-flakes falling at the wave of wizard
    wands,
While leafless branches moan and wring their with-
    ered hands.

But all those phantoms vanish now, and so I'm
    here,—
A dull old bachelor, all gaunt and gray and sere;
And that is why I sit and smoke my pipe alone,
Or watch the dying embers on my dim hearth-stone.

For when the curling whiffs of feathery smoke arise
From out their shadowy depths, I see her love-lit
    eyes;
And when I watch the embers in the ashes there,
I see the gleaming of her wondrous golden hair.

And though for home and wife and children's laugh
    I yearn,
With her my heart was buried, never to return;
And though on earth I still see many a lovely face,
No angel from the skies could take that lost one's
    place.

A FLOWER FROM THE GRAVE OF SHELLEY.

LONESOME little faded blossom,
   Nestling in a stranger's hand,
Torn from Shelly's gentle bosom,
   Banished now to this far land!

Born of Shelley's ashes holy,
   Nourished by the heart of Keats,
Under ruins melancholy,
   By the charnels' dim retreats;

Springing under arches olden,
   By the dust of queens and kings,
In the scenes of legends golden,
   And the haunts of spirit-wings!

All my heart is filled with pity
   As I gaze into thy face,—
From the old eternal city,
   Wandering to this far-off place!

But while kings and queens may perish,
   Other kings and queens are born,
And each fading flower we cherish
   Blooms again some April morn.

Tell me, then, how buds still blossom,
  And new monarchs come to reign,
While the songs from Shelley's bosom
  Never thrill the world again?

THE LITTLE WANDERER.

TELL me, pretty little maiden,
    Flitting round my footsteps slow,
Lips with love and laughter laden,
    How you reached this world below?

Bringing dreams of spring-time flowers,
    Bringing dreams of summer skies,
Bringing dreams of budding bowers,
    Blithesome birds and butterflies!

Bringing dreams of vistas vanished,
    Bringing dreams of perished years,
Bringing dreams of faces banished,
    Happy days now hid in tears!

Are you not some truant fairy
    Like a little mortal drest,
Or some bird with young wings airy
    Fluttering from your mother's nest?

Tell me, little angel vision,
    How you came to meet me here;
Did you steal from fields Elysian,
    Wandering, lost on earth, my dear?

No, my darling, you are mortal,
   Come to share our dreary dearth,—
Newly come from heaven's pearl portal,—
   Come to cheer our cheerless earth!

Leaving heaven, the angels kissed you,
   And their great, soft eyes grew dim;
Leaving heaven, they surely missed you,
   Wandering through these deserts grim!

And I fear, by envy driven,
   Pining for your face, my dear,
They will steal you back to heaven,
   Leaving us in anguish here.

But should jealous seraphs spare you,
   Sad, I fear, would be your lot;
Few would be the joys to cheer you;
   Life is cruel, little tot!

Were I but some wizard olden,
   I would deck your path with flowers
Overarched with heavens golden,
   Free from blasts and chilling showers.

Were I king, with wealth and glory,
   I would scatter at your feet
All the gems of song and story,
   Dreams of poets bright and sweet.

But these gifts are all denied me.
  So, my heart, forever true,
Prays that you may flit beside me,
  I from harm defending you.

So your little feet may never
  On a flinty pathway be,
While the darts from Sorrow's quiver,
  Missing you, shall wound but me.

"SCORN NOT THE HEART."

SCORN not the heart which may be proffered thee,
  For burning love may change to burning hate.
  When summer pineth in her queenly state,
The wan, wild autumn in her path shall be,
Blighting her blossoms as her footsteps flee;
  When day's white wings fade through her golden gate,
  The shadows gather in the gloaming late,
And shroud her splendors in the solemn sea;
When through the tropic forests's noonday warm
  The waking blasts invade the gorgeous bowers,
Their glories perish in the furious storm;
  While selfish Life holds revel through the hours,
He starts at last to see Death's awful form
    Creep, cold and cruel, through the fading flowers.

CONFIRMATION.

THE children, robed in spotless white, I see
   Kneel for a blessing at the bishop's feet,
And, as I gaze upon their faces sweet,
As pure as doves, from stain of sin so free,
Before the priest whose sins unnumbered be,
   Whose heart for selfish, sordid aims doth beat,
   I marvel why his blessing they entreat,
When he to them should rather bend the knee.

Dear little hearts, my soul adopts your creed;
   Dear little feet, your pathway I shall share;
Dear little hands, my wanderings ye shall lead!
   Dear little brows, guide with your golden hair;
Dear little lips, my God's forgiveness plead;
   Dear little eyes, shine on my soul's despair!

"MARY."

OF all the sweet names that ever were given
    To mortals on earth or seraphs in heaven,
No matter if borne by milkmaid or fairy,
The sweetest of all must ever be " Mary."

There's "Helen," the star of song and of story,
Men perished to wreathe her ringlets with glory;
There also is " Ruth," so true and so tender,
Whose meekness and faith make strong men sur-
    render.

And " Mabel " 's a name that ever sounds sweetly,
And charms and enchants a mortal completely,
While " Katie " suggests brown eyes and brown
    tresses,
Created for love and lover's caresses.

There's " Maud" with a mouth as red as a cherry,
With kisses so sweet, with laughter so merry;
There's " Edith," whose eyes are blue as the
    fountains,
With ringlets of gold like morn on the mountains.

There's " Blanche," and " Adele," that sound
    autocratic,
Poor " Sarah " and " Jane " that dwell in an attic,

While "Emma" is dear, all dote upon "Jenny,"
And "Annie" is loved not least among many.

But never a name like "Mary" is spoken;
The dearest of dreams revive at that token,
Each other brings joy or brightness or sweetness,
But "Mary" alone has perfect completeness.

The lady high-born who reigns in a castle,
The widow forlorn, the spouse of the vassal,
The captive chained down in dungeon cell dreary,
The diademed queen, may bear the name "Mary."

And "Mary"'s the soul who opes the heart's
    portals,
A sweetheart, perchance, the dearest of mortals;
A sister, whose soul is dowered with beauty,
Or mother, who lives for love and for duty.

'Twas "Mary" who first shed tears of contrition,
'Twas she who was blest with God's greatest mis-
    sion;
She stood by His cross, she saw His tomb riven,
Her name shall be first on earth and in heaven.

"BACK TO THE WORLD."

BACK to the world, with all its toils and tears,
    My faltering footsteps once again must turn.
  The one for whom my sad soul still would yearn,
Through weary months and dreary, dreary years,
With ever-struggling hosts of hopes and fears,
    At last with careless tongue my love doth spurn,
    And while I with my cruel anguish burn,
My one sweet dream forever disappears.

Within the crystal goblet's purple gleam
    My soul strives to forget her starry eyes;
Within the great world's swiftly-surging stream
    My heart heaves to escape her sweet, strong ties;
Yet though deep buried, well I know my dream
    Will haunt me with a grief that never dies.

FRAGMENTS
FROM
"THE OUTCAST AND OTHER POEMS"
1885

MORNING.

I SEE the morning in ebon east,
   And catch the glitter of her silver spears;
And now she rises in her royal robes
Of purple and of scarlet flecked with gold,
Like an enchantress on her bridal day,
Who waits to welcome some enamored king,
Or as an Arab princess decked with gems,
And all the fabled splendors of Arabian tales.

EVENING.

THE creamy cloudlets, like a flock of swans,
   Are floating on their flaky wings of white
See monstrous mists arising in the north
Like snowy mountains in the Arctic seas,
Until the splendor of the dying day
Has glorified them like the heights of heaven
With walls of jasper and with domes of gold;
At last the stately Sun falls in his grave,
And then like dusky Titans thunderstruck,
The giant phantoms sink behind the hills.

AUTUMN.

DEPARTING summer lingers sadly still
    Around the faded field and misty hill;
The quaking branches of the bare trees sigh
And chilly rains fall where the dead leaves lie;
The brambles grow where blushing roses bloomed
And nightshade spreads where lilies lie entombed;
The mournful spirit of the Autumn treads
Where yellow asters hang their withered heads.

The birds of passage, faintly calling, fly
To seek a home beneath a southern sky;
Amid the rustling woods at pensive eve
The waving mists their sombre fabrics weave;
The sinking sun amid the mottled skies
Spreads through the cold gray clouds his burning
      dyes,
And scarlet streamers flame around his bier
With awful glories of the waning year.

And now I tread the lonesome garden walks
Beside the dry, decaying lily stalks,
Amid deserted, drooping yellow bowers
Bent with their blighted buds and faded flowers
And see amid the numb November gloom
The radiance of a lone Magnolia bloom,

In spotless splendor soon to pass away
Amid this desolation and decay;

Like one who met me under skies of May,
And still is mine, while others pass away,
When spring and summer long have left my heart,
And false friends, like my false hopes, all depart,—
To linger with me through the blast and blight
And through the shadows of the coming night,
Yet falters at the setting of my sun,
And then forsakes me as the rest have done.

THREE SOUTHERN SCENES.

I.

THE SAVANNAH.

WE ride through forests ever cool and green,
    Where giant live-oaks join their boughs above,
All knit together by a thousand vines,
The trumpet flower, with its blazing blooms
Whose martial music flashes into flame,
The brier, bramble and the poison oak,
Like scaly serpents thrusting forth their fangs,
While spiders, like the Sirens long ago,
Spread silken snares bedecked with dazzling dew
To tangle in the feet of foolish flies;
Through treacherous fens and wastes of matted shrubs,
Above the black mould, ever dank and cold
Burst through by lushy clumps of whitened sprouts,
Where lies concealed the deadly rattlesnake;
By greenly-mantled ponds, made beautiful
With multitudes of water lilies white.

And then a blue lake shimmers in the sun
Or quivers in the gloomy cypress shades;
A gorgeous wild duck floats upon the waves
With plumage polished like a coat of mail;
The snakes are twisted on the rotten limbs

Of dead trees that have fallen in the lake;
On yonder logs, the turtles in a line
Are drying broad backs in the burning sun;
The blue jay, like a noisy trooper, calls,
The red bird flutters like a flower of flame;
The gaunt gar, like a Turkish scimitar,
Leaps from the lake, and circling sinks from sight.

II.

AN AUTUMN MORNING.

A RICH October morning, calm and still,
When saddened skies hang in a dreamy haze;
The red and yellow leaves dance in the light,
Arraying every hill in regal robes.
The flocks of squirrels gather ripening nuts,
The luscious wild grapes in blue clusters cling,
And bright woodpeckers whisk amid the leaves.
The dry broom-sedge grows over wasted fields
Fringing red gullies and rough banks of clay;
Along the highway and the meadows brown
The golden-rods and asters are ablaze.

Here stands a planter's house amid his farms
Of snowy cotton and of golden corn,
Specked here and there by low-roofed negro huts
Whose dusky denizens in fleecy fields
Sing with a sweet mysterious melody
The songs of Salem in this western world
With all the fervor of its ancient bards.

Far, far above, amid the dreamy skies
The buzzards glide on still and stately wings,
While birds of passage, in a bending line
Fly from the far north to the southern seas.

III.

THE OLD MANSION.

I SEE a ghostly ruin of the past
  And tread its cedar-bordered avenues.
Around its porticoes the pillars tall
Stand like a row of trusty sentinels
Guarding the glories of a perished race
Amid its desolation and decay;
A few tall roses and magnolias stand
Around a fountain choked with water weeds.

See the great rooms, whose mirrored walls are
  crushed
And marble mantles now are overthrown.
My footstep falling in the haunted halls,
Seems waking from the dead and dusty years
The far-off echoes of a hunter's horn
Blown by the master of a thousand slaves;
Amid the shadows of this archway old
I see a beauteous high-born lady stand
And hear the rustle of her silken gown;
Amid the broken mirrors on the walls
The softest brown eyes ever seen on earth
Shine on me from their dewy, dusky depths

With starry splendors of a tropic night;
My whisper, stealing through the ruined rooms
Brings back the laughter of the yester-years,
And all the revels of a nuptial night,
Until the dead bride from her mossy tomb
Comes treading by me in her robes of white;
Amid the cobwebs on the ancient stair,
I see the shimmer of her snowy veil,
The withered orange blossoms on her brow,
And then, her sweet face swiftly vanishing
Amid the glimmer of her golden hair.

TO ONE DEPARTED

THY loving work is done forevermore,
    Thy tender heart is free from all its cares,
For at the coming of the still, sad night,
Thy folded hands have won their final rest.
So thou art drawing near thy happy home,
With gladsome singing and with golden sheaves,
Fearing no foe amid the gloom of death,
Seeing beyond the radiant wings of dawn,
The plumy palm trees of a paradise
With pearly portals and with gates of gold.

Thy happy days, my dearest, have begun,
While we on earth are still amid our woes;
We can not dream of half thy boundless bliss,
Our deepest joy would be a pain to thine;
Thou wert the fairest flower of the earth
And now heaven claims thee as its loveliest star.

THE CYNIC.

IN festal halls the flaring lights hang round,
    And artificial beauty flaunts beneath;
The flaming wine leaps wildly in the blood,
And artificial mirth writhes on the lips;
The noisy music thrills with painful joy,
And smiles of love have bale as well as bliss.
Outside, the city—huddled den of sin,—
Is boiling like a witch's caldron in the night.

And here the cynic treads to scoff and jeer
At beauty, sweetness and at innocence;
Their gentle smiles and eager, loving eyes
Are blasted as he rudely passes by.
His laughter is an agonizing spasm,
And bears a likeness unto wholesome mirth
As yellow autumn leaflets, sick and sere,
Are like the tender foliage of the spring.

Then, should he tread where fragrant garden flowers
Breathe out their odors like a song from heaven,
He carries with him artificial blight
And drouth and dearth, to kill them like a curse.
So, like a thorn-tree, battered, bruised and worn,
He multiplies his thorns for every wound,
Or like the proud Egyptian queen of old
He hugs a serpent that shall sting his soul.

A STORM IN SUMMER.

THE August sun blazed with a blasting heat
    And on the yellowing corn-fields fiercely beat,
The sky was burning with an ashen blue
And glaring with the hot beams darting through;
The hazy dust was rising everywhere
And floating slowly on the stifling air.
All day the katydid chirped sharp and shrill
And green grasshoppers answered from the hill;
Deep in the lushy grass the cricket purred
While in the trees all day the locust whirred;
All night the dry-flies from the dusky limbs
Ground forth their sawing, nasal-twanging hymns.

Sometimes we watched the reapers in the field
In a long line their flashing sickles wield.
We hunted for the quail's nest through the wheat
And found it hidden, quiet, snug and neat.
A nest of grass, filled full of snowy spheres,
Thick as the grains upon the ripened ears,
Pure as the pearls that gleam in Indian seas
Or milk-white buds upon the locust trees.

Then after weary waiting came the rain
When panting earth grew fresh and green again.
The morning ere the rain was red and hot
And like sharp arrows sultry sunbeams shot.

A Storm in Summer.

But when noon came the breeze began to blow
Delicious coolness through the feverish glow;
And then from out the west dull clouds arose
And skimmed along, too restless for repose.
More clouds began to follow, till they grew
Darker and broader, while the strong winds blew.
Soon deep-toned thunder echoed from the clouds,
And sword-like flashes drove the mists in crowds.
Ah, how delicious to the eager ear
Were those cool shadows, swiftly drawing near!
It seemed unto the anxious farmer's mind,
That loftiest music rode upon the wind.
It seemed as if the God of manly sport
With horns and hounds had come to hold his court,
Returned through faded earth to rove at will
And caper gladly o'er the yellowing hill;
To shout and laugh amid reviving flowers,
And drive his baying hounds through forest bowers.

The clouds grew blacker, till they loomed like night,
And then the blasts came roaring in their might;
The mighty elms were swayed from side to side,
For like a devil did the tempest ride.
The oaks groaned and their mighty limbs were crushed;
The rafters creaked as by the roofs he rushed.

And now, upon the mountain's distant side,
A shroud-like sheet of rain was seen to glide;
Then soon the valleys at its feet were crossed,

And nearer, nearer by, the fields were lost:
Next, the hard gust came with a mighty stride,—
The driving rain was scattered far and wide!
Yes, there it was at last in all its strength,
And fast was filling all the country's length;
It came as in an overwhelming flood,
And drenched the meadow and the field and wood.

All through the storm we nestled on the hay
That, piled in huge heaps, through the barn-rooms lay;
The tempest flooded all the roof without,
And great gusts shook the rafters with a shout.
Far up above, the mud-flies worked away,
Building their cells of well-cemented clay;
The little wren within her nook peered out,
And squeaking mice would slyly skip about;
The lithe, slim swallow fluttered on her nest,
Her chattering fledglings robbing her of rest.

At last the rain ceased, and the clouds flew by,
Showing the dark blue of the dewy sky;
Upon the outskirts of the dying storm
The glorious rainbow reared his regal form;
But soon the winds tore down the fragile arch,
As frosty footsteps through the roses march.

"THE BEGINNING OF THE END."

POOR helpless child, sleep softly through the night,
For on thy heart to-morrow falls the blight;
Sleep on in all thy peaceful thoughtlessness,
And dream the last time of thy youthful bliss;
For with the coming of the hapless day
A shadow falls, to never pass away.
Would thou couldst shun the path thou soon must wend,
Would that thy sleep could never have an end.
Soon comes the glitter of the morning light,
But morning brings thee everlasting night.

Joy seems amid thy cherub cheeks to smile,
And in thy dimples basks a little while;
But soon thy timid face will hotly flame
With branded hues of deep and lasting shame;
Within thy heart a guilty secret lies,
The serpent of a sin that never dies;
For thou hast loved too much and loved too well
And fallen helpless in a fearful spell;
Thy lover now hath left thee all alone,
And soon thy deadly secret shall be known.
He leaves thee, with an aching heart of lead,
To wander when thy happy hopes are dead,

"The Beginning of the End."

To nurse a being not from wedlock sprung
Which headless passion from thy bosom wrung,
A helpless soul to bear an outcast's name,
Proof of thy guilt and witness of thy shame.

Thee, crouching from the cruel lash I see
Upon the plowshares where thy path shall be,
Thy soft feet bleeding on the pointed flint,
And eyes more cruel fiercely o'er thee bent—
Those childish feet too fair for violet beds,
White as the leaves the dying lily sheds!
Then, darling, in the dust I see thee hurled,
Amid the curses of a cruel world,
And as thou crouchest, hiding from its wrath,
I see thy spoiler tread his primrose path,
And, spitting on his victim fallen down,
The world rewards the traitor with a crown.

MARTYRDOM.

THE martyr need not perish by the gallows, at
    the stake, or cross-tree high;
For often it is nobler and is braver for his creed to
    live than die.

THE POET.

AMID the blossoms, under skies of blue,
    The brown bee seeks and gathers honey-
    dew;
The poet seeks through glory and through gloom
And gathers beauty both in blight and bloom.

BEFORE THE BATTLE.

AROUND me spread ten thousand camps of
    white,
So wide they cover all the distant hills
Like the vast flocks of some barbaric tale
The giant Cyclops folded round their caves.

THE BATTLE.

AT first a few blasts shake the startled air,
And then a hundred burst in serried flame,
While all the Earth is quaking in its fear
And all the hills are rocking to their base.
The iron balls are rushing, crushing by,
And all is ruin where they quiver past;
They scatter leaves like fierce December winds,
And giant trees come crashing to the ground;
The stones are splintered high upon the hills,
The sod is ploughed, the sky is dim with dust;
The baleful bombs are bursting far and near
And frightened echoes answer back the sounds;
It seems as if the ancient days of Earth
Have now returned with all their giant brood,
And all the Titans, hurled from lofty heaven,
Are struggling with the Thunderer on his throne.

THE SPRING.

I SEE above us, from a mossy wall,
   A bubbling spring leap in a broken fall;
Its torrents dash upon the jutting rocks,
And splashing outward, shiver with the shocks;

Its silver cascade breaks in brilliant bars,
Or twinkles like a maze of sparkling stars,
Shooting its dewdrops like a shower of gems,
Till all the ferns are decked with diadems.

The water lilies glimmer through the glooms,
The graceful grasses lift their princely plumes,
The velvet mosses on the boulders brown
Make for the idler softest couch of down.

The caverns underneath are all so cool,
So peaceful is the smooth, rush-bordered pool,
One seems to tread beneath the subtle spell
Of some sweet nymph who rules the crystal well.

PATRIOTISM.

IF your victorious sword in foeman's heart finds
    sheath,
The world comes forth to crown you with a laurel
    wreath;
But if you fall, no matter how you fight and bleed,
It spits upon your corpse and crowns you with a
    weed.

MARCH.

THE wild March wind above the hilltop swells,
    And fills with withered leaves the hollow
    dells;
The hooded buds upon the haggard trees
Like little babes wrapped from the biting breeze
Hang tiny heads of brown, while bleak winds beat
And bind them with a crystal crust of sleet.

Clothed in a forest of ancestral elms
With curving limbs and lithe and lissome stems,
The hills seem shuddering in their loneliness,
Stripped of their emerald-tufted summer dress,
And from their windy tops look sadly down
Upon the meadows bare and smooth and brown.

A FATHER'S CURSE.

IF one should ever harm my helpless child,
   God grant the spoiler may be stricken down;
His wicked hopes all blasted in their bud
To bear the burden of a deadly fruit;
Then may his cheeks be scarred with seams of sin,
And disappointment twist his wrinkled brow;
May hideous nightmares haunt him in his sleep
And choke and strangle as he strives to scream,
Or come like snakes to crawl within his bed,
And on his breast in cold and clamy coils.
May all his love, like some red poison flower
Conceal a scorpion a deadly sting,
Or like a flame above a reeking fen
Allure him onward to his place in hell.

THE ONE THING NEEDFUL."

THERE is but one bliss left of paradise,—
   That is to know our love has been returned;
When weary cares will vanish in a kiss,
   And gentle hands will heal where hate hath burned.
Mere friendship by itself is but a name,
   Fulfilled ambition but an empty show,
The heart a dead rose, faded from its flame,
   A nest deserted, filled with winter snow.

IN PARADISE.

How sweet must be thy bowers, bedecked in never-fading blooms,
Thy fountains sparkling under spicy forests ever green,
Beyond the desolation of this solemn waste of tombs,
In stately splendor that shall never by mine eyes be seen.

Each year a band departs that binds me closer unto thee;
Each year my path grows darker as I lose them one by one;
And looking from their blooming isles of joy, they pity me,
Amid Earth's fading autumn bowers, so chilly, dark and lone.

STANZAS TO MADELINE.

I DO not love thee for thy queenly grace,
   Nor all thy blooming beauties, which outshine
The stars that twinkle round the full moon's face,
   Or roseate splendors of the day's decline.

For dearest, thou art good and true and sweet,
   And when I take thy gentle hand in mine,
I trust to thee to guide my faltering feet.
   Through gloom or glory, with thy love divine.

Through radiant noons, and sombre shades of eve
   When golden sunbeams perish in the night,
Around my eager heart thy soft spells weave
   Enchanted fancies full of deep delight.

Thy words of kindness in my bosom glow,
   So golden summer decks in sweeter bloom,
Or, when the winter night is chill with snow,
   The flying winds sing sweetly through the gloom.

CALLISTA

AGAINST the flinty rocks the wild waves clash,
From sable clouds the fitful lightnings flash,
And in the rocking tempest, far on high
The scattered flocks of sea-birds homeward fly,—
But I heed not the storm-clouds as they roll,
For deeper darkness covers all my soul.

Why can not I protect thee from the storm?
Curst be the blast that beats thy tender form!
Before thou lov'dst me, happiness was thine,
Thy life not snared within the woes of mine;
Thy wert a bud born on a summer day
Where winter winds were never known to stray.

But now from out thy garden cast, to die,
I see thee with thy bleeding bosom lie,
Thy shining locks bedabbled with the rain,
Thy sweet lips sprinkled with a crimson stain,
A white-robed figure with a face of woe,
Amid the blackness, pale and cold as snow.

In vain I clasp thee to my bosom warm,
In vain I press thy pallid, pulseless form;
The lightnings flash so I can see thy face,
And awful anguish there hath left its trace;
I see amid the glitter of their light
The red wound dripping from thy breasts of white.

Callista, darling, I have murdered thee
Beside the wild waves of the sobbing sea;
And hast thou left me, sweet, forevermore?—
'Twas for the best that cruel wound I tore,—
Yes for the best, but I am wild with pain,—
Callista, wilt thou not return again?

Thou knowest all the maddening love I feel,
Which made me in thy bosom drive the steel.
The hated bridegroom came across the sea
To take the love that was alone for me;
The feast was set, the music pealed thy doom,
His sails were set to bear thee to his home.

We fled, and on our flight his minions hung,
But by my side my darling closely clung,
For like blood-hounds they yelled in sight behind
And sought to seize thee in mine arms entwined.
How I remember now thy piteous cries,
While clinging to my neck with streaming eyes!

I did not wait, my dagger flashed like fire,—
I saw its wrath within thy heart expire!
Thy lips half opened in a piteous cry,
And then I saw thee on my bosom die;
Then, when they saw thee perish from my wrath,
They dared not follow on my fearful path.

The foreign hawk must seize some other bride,
He can not, shall not, tear thee from my side!

I slew thee and I slew my soul with thee,
But still thou art no slave, thy heart is free!
Nor will I have to curse the despot's band
That might have bound thee in his hapless land.

Callista, thou art now an angel blest,
While I must wander without hope or rest,
Beautiful heaven is thy happy home,
While I, an exile, still on earth must roam;
O, seraph maiden, on thy starry throne,
Behold me, I am friendless and alone!

To-morrow will the sun rise fair again,
But for thy lover it will rise in vain.
The songs of spring shall never sooth my grief,
My heart shall wither like an autumn leaf;
My pathway, once bestrewn with summer blooms,
Shall lead forever through a waste of tombs.

ON A LOCK OF MARIE ANTOINETTE'S HAIR,

Placed beside one from the head of the Dauphin, at the New Orleans Centennial.

HERE in this bustling western world of ours
    Thou liest lonely as the throngs pass by,
Like some bright bloom torn from its native bowers,
    Or hapless peri banished from on high.
Shorn from the regal head long years ago,
    Thy golden playmates to the grave all given—
A plume dropped from an angel's wing below
    When turning in an upward flight to heaven.

I ponder long upon the tearful tale
    Of her the fairest flower of her day—
A song of triumph ending in a wail,
    A throb of gladness lost in deep dismay.
Wherever I may tread it haunts me still
    When snowflakes fall or vernal blossoms blow,
A tale that makes the brightest eyes to fill,
    That beauty like thine ever leads to woe.

I see the splendors of the Austrian court,
    And she its jewel and its morning star,
Surrounded by a hundred frowning forts
    And all the splendor and the state of war.

I see her now decked as a monarch's bride,
    A queenly rose in all her radiant charms;
Two mighty nations turn to her in pride
    Beneath their banners and emblazoned arms.

Again I see her when the furious mob
    Whose myriad grizzled faces writhe and glow,
Has blanched her cheek and wrung forth many a sob
    Till all her golden locks are white as snow.
And then the last scene comes before mine eyes
    When Death has draped her in his fatal veil;
I see the scaffold in the darkness rise
    Where stands the headsman with his glittering steel.

And here beside the mother's strands of gold
    I see the little Dauphin's silken hair,
As close as when she would her boy enfold
    Before the coming of her last despair.
I see the frantic flashing of her eyes
    When he is torn from out her eager arms;
I hear her prayers and her piercing cries
    While clinging to him in her fierce alarms;

Then, like a tigress brought at last to bay,
    Her furious anguish drives her on her foes;
But soon they snatch her pretty boy away
    And leave her sinking in despairing throes.

On a Lock of Marie Antoinette's Hair.

Thou couldst not then one manly champion find,
   Since every fate had plotted to destroy;
Else thousands would have died and called to mind
   Another Helen and another Troy.

I see thee in the dwellings of the dead
   By Cleopatra, thrilled with piercing pangs,
Whose beauteous breast, an asp has made his bed,
   Sucking her nipples with his fiery fangs.
And there beside thee is the lovely maid
   Whose dagger slew the fierce, unnatural sire,
And Mary Stewart, by the headsman's blade
   That quenched in night her heart's impassioned fire.

DELIA.

HER sparkling eyes are like two drops of dew
    That twinkle under summer skies of blue,
Her cheeks like lilies flushed by dawn of day,
Her sweet mouth sweeter than the month of May;
Her little blue-veined feet, so soft, so swift,
That from the earth her figure seem to lift,
So white, so airy, free from spot and stain,
Are like the doves that wafted Cupid's wain;
Her bosom's like the cloud by morning spun,
Decked in the roses of the rising sun,
And on her swelling, gently-heaving breast
White-wingéd Love hath built his happy nest.

No other maiden lives in hut or hall
Nor ever breathed since Eve's and Adam's fall
To vie with her in gentleness and grace;
And she outshines them with her lovely face,
As gladsome summer, warm with fragrant flowers,
Outshines cold autumn's gaudy, lifeless bowers,
As radiant stars in jeweled skies outshine
The stony gems set in a chilly mine.

MORTALITY.

MINE eyes behold an old man's callous corpse
    With grizzled hair and wrinkled cheeks and
        brows;
I wonder if he lost or won the race of life,
And if he earned its glory or disgrace;—
No matter now, for it is all the same
Were this dead man a pauper or a prince.

I know not if in far, hot-blooded youth,
He revelled in its sweet forbidden joys,
When woman and when wine were Sin's first snares,
And Sin herself was beautiful and bright
Before her form grew hideous in the end;—
If so, he learned, as others, that those joys
When at their height are but akin to pain.

I know not if he trod through Virtue's ways
The dull, dry desert of our common life;—
If so, no angel came to crown his brow,
Nor cometh now to bear him to the skies.—

A WISH.

I LONG to see thee, dearest, as of yore,
  And find thee happy as in perished years;
To see the smile upon thy warm, sweet mouth
Play like a sunbeam round a budding rose;
To see the blushes blooming through the snows
Amid the cherub dimples of thy cheek;
To see thy soft eyes haunt my steps again
Like glorious velvet wingéd butterflies.

But I have lost thee, and thy face, my love,
Seems like an angel's at the gate of heaven,
When, watching for a loved one left on earth,
And after waiting weary, weary years,
It sees its darling counted with the lost.

THE BARD.

IF on your brow should rest the poet's bays,
  Your feet must tread on thistles all your days;

If Poesie should bid you share her bliss,
Her lips will sting you when they give a kiss;

And though your heart and harp should ring in rhyme
As the doe's heart beats with her mate's in time,

At last, a deer that hears the bloodhound's bay,
Your heart grows mad with passions fierce for prey;

And then your harp-strings sigh for joys of yore,
As chill winds sigh when summer days are o'er;

Too late, too late! If you the laurels wear,
Think not to trip through fields and forests fair;

For you must tread through famine, fire and flood,
And write your poems from your own heart's blood.

FRAGMENTS
FROM
"CLARIBEL AND OTHER POEMS."
1882

TO MY LITTLE NIECE,
ALMA VERNEY MALONE,
I INSCRIBE THESE VERSES
OF MY CHILDHOOD.

INEZ.

I SEE her on a crimson velvet seat
　At midnight, in a hall encircled round
With dazzling lights that glare with eyes of fire
Upon her as she reigns above them all,
A hundred lords and ladies of degree.

Not like the haughty dame, whose queenly form
Seems chiseled out of arctic ice and snow;
With golden tresses and with azure eyes
Above a bosom white as water lilies,
So that she seems the spirit of the spring.
Returning through the winter's kingdom white,
With sunshine and with velvet violets,—
No, hers the beauty of the Persian maid
Which Oriental lovers hold so dear.
Her face is like a yellow crocus bloom,
Or like the golden orange of the South,
And when the red blush mantles to her cheeks,
She seems the setting of a summer sun
In the soft bosom of a rosy cloud.

A cactus blossom in her sable hair
Gives to the gloomy grandeur of its night
The scarlet splendor of a setting star.

Ah, sweet enchantress of the passionate South,
You chain your victims with a chain of gold;
But close to you I see a lover stand,
His jealous hand upon his dagger's hilt,
His dark face scowling there beside your own,—
A cobra and a gorgeous tropic flower.

REALIZED HOPES.

DESIRES dear to our souls, that come to pass
Have more deceit than those which disappoint,
And heartfelt hopes, when in the end fulfilled,
Bring more heart-sickness than the hopes that fail.

DESPAIR.

CAN a drop raise the ocean? A wren's feather
Add weight unto the world? A moment's time
Add to the length of God's eternity?
Can death add one more pang to this numb heart
Whose shadows are so deep their lightest hue
Is darker than the plume the vulture wears
Amid far-off enchanted spirit lands;
Whose silence is terrific as the tomb
That hides the wreck of undone Babylon;
Whose pangs are like a scream in haunted halls
In some dire, rocking storm, at midnight-time;
Whose sleep no drug can add nightmare unto;
Whose whole self is a grave, like Egypt's realms
Strewn with the ruins of a thousand years;
Which never from the charnel shall arise,
Or feel the morning star above the awful waste?

THE COMING OF APRIL.

IN gardens of green young April is queen;
    She scatters the winter snows;
Like a blithesome boy, with laughter and joy,
    She banishes worldly woes.
She treadeth the earth with music and mirth,
    Her lap overflowing with sweets,
With daffodillies and valley lilies
    And showers in silver sheets;
With blushing roses, narcissus posies,
    The velvet greensward to illume,
And the hyacinth from its curly plinth,
    The sweetest flower that ever breathed perfume.

Like the green sea-waves are the forest leaves,
    As they dance in the morning breeze,
And they quiver and bound with a merry sound
    To the boom of the honeybees.
Then the bounteous earth is giving birth
    To wonderful worlds of life;
On each warm clod of the generous sod
    Begins an eager strife;
For the bursting germs and the prisoned worms
    Feel their deliverance nigh,—
To rise in bowers of purple flowers
    And many a butterfly.

The Coming of April.

In the bounding billows of the waving willows
    The quaint little fairies hide,
And in garlanded glooms and in budding blooms
    By the peeping birds are spied;
On the fragrant lawn the satyr and faun
    Skip, laughing at themselves;
Then the tender sheaves of the opening leaves
    And the rosebuds cradle the baby elves;
Through the morning hours, in the lilac flowers
    The Zephyr doth flutter in flight,
And down in the waves the lovely nymph laves,
    Whirling her arms of white;
And swirling and swinging and laughing and singing
    On the blossoming boughs of the tufted trees,
The dryad reclines in the tangled vines,
    Her yellow hair a-waving in the breeze.

And the birds themselves are but tiny elves
    Disguised with a beak and feather,
To banish our sadness with songs of their gladness,
    Through sunny or snowy weather;
See the quaint little queen with her eggs of green,
    Of ivory white, or of blue and gold,
In a nest of down or of leaflets brown,
    Where her pearls into life shall unfold!

How changeful the ways of April's days!
    Sunshine and storm, storm and sunshine
Fleetly descending are sweetly blending
    From the violet vale to the mountain pine.

Like a maiden in love she blushes above
   Or smiles with a downcast glance,
Then shows by a start the love of her heart,
   Yet fearing to advance;
Pretending to detest the one she loves best,
   And pouting in his face,
Now timid and coy, now bubbling with joy,
   And leading her lover a chase.

We never know why, but often we sigh
   In the April hours sweet;
For beauty and gladness tread ever with sadness,
   And never apart those three we meet;
So, with hand in hand, and from land to land,
     Through the morning light and the noon-day glow,
Under footsteps fleet bringing bitter and sweet
   They scatter bliss and woe.
When the blithe bird notes from the tiny trilling throats
   Quiver or tremble or dance through the air,
When the flowers consume their lives in perfume,
   They oppress our souls with care;—
A lonesome unrest that leaps in the breast,
   Cloying alike a voluptuous vision,
Like the piercing bliss of love's first kiss,
   Too thrilling but for spirits elysian.

Soon April has flown and left us alone
   In the fields of the fading year;

The garlands she gathered are blighted and withered,
   And her bowers are silent and sere;
Her bird songs are banished, her flowers are vanished
   In the sultry summer heat;
Then stern winter blows his whirlwind of snows
   And fetters with frost and sleet.

So when love has departed, we roam broken-hearted,
   Through a passionate torrid zone,
And dreams of the past, too lovely to last,
   Shall leave us in winter alone.

THE HUMMING-BIRD.

I FLIT through the bowers of April flowers
    And the mellow skies of June,
O'er sparkling floods and bloomy woods,
    From orient morn to radiant noon.
From the fairy cells of budding bells
    I suck the golden honey;
They sway and they swing at the wave of my wing,
    And my fires make shadows sunny.
Unknown to pain and earthly stain,
    I glitter near and far:
My courses I run, like a beam from the sun,
    Or a midnight shooting star.

In the torrid zone my fires are sown,
    And in northern worlds of ice,
Over wizard strands in the arctic lands
    And the palmy isles of paradise.
Where the awful night in winter bedight
    Shrouds desolate, boundless seas,
I glint through the glooms with butterfly plumes
    When the mariner despairing flees;
The dark-eyed maiden of the southern Eden
    Far, far from the kingdom of snows,
Will give me a smile as I bask awhile
    In the heart of a tropic rose.

No mortal sorrow, no fear of the morrow
   Can darken my rainbow hours,
Though the bale be thine, the bliss shall be mine;
   I live forever in budding flowers;
When the buds I cherished have pined and have perished,
   I fly to the younger blooms;
I know not the dearth of this lone earth,
   Nor the shades of its silent tombs;
By the angels given, I flutter from heaven,
   I can not abide in a cage,
I beat at my bars to soar to the stars
   Till I die in restless rage.

A WINTER MIDNIGHT.

THE huge snowflakes seem shaking phantom wings,
And now the wind a song of madness sings;
The haggard branches croon a runic verse
And wave their wild wands in a wizard curse.

OPPORTUNITY.

ONE fateful hour may be life's diadem,
　　Each of its moments be a precious gem;
Then grasp the jewels ere the door be shut,
Lest thou shouldst lose thy palace for a hut.

THE VICTOR.

WHEN Love shall be her sword, her virtue, shield,
The timid maiden wins on every field.

LOVE AFTER DEATH.

IF in the life to come our ways should part,
　　My feet should seek forever for my queen
And I would come to clasp her to my heart
　　Though fifty worlds were interposed between.

ONE SUMMER.

THE thorns upon this world of ours
   Sometimes bud forth in gentle flowers;
Where night has made our earth forlorn
Will rise at last a radiant morn;
On this short journey to the tomb
Some thrilling voice will break the gloom;
But Youth and Love when once passed by
Leave all our dearest hopes to die;
Their piercing joy and blissful pain
Once felt, are never felt again.

A sojourn at a farm in June,
When fields were fresh and woods in tune,
When bare existence was a joy
To me, a fond and foolish boy!
Ah yes, my dream of love was done,
At setting of that summer sun!

Ah, little modest country maid,
Doomed with the summer day to fade,
Too fragile and too fair to last,
Lost flower of the happy past!
I see you still beside me here,
Just as you looked that bygone year.
Your sweet face smiles within my reach
Amid pink blossoms of the peach,

Or wreathed with wild grapes from the wood,
Your cheeks stained with their purple blood
Or rising like a pure, pale flower
Amid a scarlet poppy bower.

I see you still with eyes of blue,
The darkest pansy's deepest hue;
Your brown hair gently wavers down
And glimmers like a copper crown·
A basket on your arm you bear,
An awkward little bonnet wear;
Fresh as the dewy wildwoods green,—
My little sweetheart, and my queen!

Her goodness warms misfortune's dearth
And makes a heaven out of earth;
Singing she cooks the scanty meal,
Or chatting, turns the creaking wheel;
With hoe and huge straw hat, she leads
Destructive war against the weeds,
Till I, a dapper city clerk,
Begin to help her with her work,
And sometimes try to milk her cows,
Or with her drive them out to browse.

She tells me names of birds and trees,
And habits of the honeybees,
She shows me where blackberries grow·
And where the pink wild roses blow.
She sits with me in mossy nooks
Of sylvan shades and bubbling brooks.

And then we see the red-bird shy,
A blazing blossom, flutter by
And proudly shake his crimson plumes
And chirp amid the verdant glooms;
The brown thrush, of a humbler crest,
With calm eyes watches from her nest.
We roam beside the deep green pools
In which the bulfrog blithly rules
And leaps among the daffodillies,
Blue flags and snowy water lilies.

With her I watch the evening star
Begin to tremble from afar,
The moon arising in the night
And robing all the world in white;
Then, when the mock-bird, sweet and wild,—
The forest's untamed poet-child,—
Begins to twitter trills of bliss,
I snare my sweetheart with a kiss!

But Autumn comes with footsteps chilly,
And slays the blue-bell and the lily;
The purple and the golden asters wave
Above the pansy's lonely grave.
I leave her, and I turn once more,
To see her weeping at her door.
And then another look,—the last,
When dying day is nearly past;
Her hands are curved above her eyes
That watch me like two jealous spies;

The setting sunbeams light her hair,
Then leave her in her lone despair;
She lingers still until the night
Shuts her forever from my sight.

Amid the dust and roar and heat
That choke the city's crowded street,
I see her looking to the town
Across the autumn fields of brown,
Towards a happier, higher life,
Than waits the future farmer's wife,
While heartless fortune holds her down,
And mates her with a common clown.

Ah, precious little country girl,
Who beamed forlorn, an ocean pearl,
A sweet, low-waving wildwood rose,
Frail poem in a world of prose!

Again I ponder all alone,
While snowflakes fall and bleak winds moan,
And hear the tread of restless feet
Along the city's dingy street,
And yearn to see her face again
To ease my aching heart of pain,—
Returning from the Long Ago
Beyond her silent shroud of snow!

TRIBUTE TO SHELLEY.

HE was the son of Beauty and of Love,
   Born in the lilies of the land of dreams;
A blithesome boy, who wandered from his home
In all his sweetness and his innocence,
And brought to earth mellifluous melodies,
Sung by the song-birds in its wondrous woods;
The gladsome singer of the summer hours,
The fair-haired playmate of the budding blooms,
Who flitted like a shadow from our sight
Amid our autumn's waste of withered leaves.

O, wondrous child, thine innocence hath power
To soar to heights where sages can not tread,
Thy sweetness thrills the cheerless heart of earth,
With strains triumphant of a starry lyre;
Our poets bring us fading flowers of earth,
Thou bearest blossoms from the fields of heaven.

His heart was deathless, but his form was dust,
His breath is still and he will sing no more!
It seemed the fire that lived within his heart
Should warm his breast within the frozen ground,
So that the Earth would throb within her womb
And give new birth unto her fairest son,
Just as the violets of the fragrant spring
Are withered but to rise as fair again.

But only lowly buds again can bloom;
When angels fall they fall to rise no more,
And stars once darkened, never beam again.

But he shall dwell in lovelier lands than this,
Low Earth he leaves to reign in Paradise,—
A land of lilies and a land of love,
Rich with the roses of eternal day,
Beyond the woes of this poor world of ours,
Beyond the splendors of the radiant morn,
Where love doth live unchanged, unharmed by time
And where the canker touches not the flower.

I am left here in loneliness and pain,
Condemned to sing such humble songs as this,
To yearn for power that is all his own;
Where all our best songs crave for nobler things,—
Whose mortal rage, chained down, laments our fate,—
The common wailings of all hearts together.
But I am happy if my loving hands
Can add one jewel to his sparkling crown.

www.ingramcontent.com/pod-product-compliance
Lightning Source LLC
Chambersburg PA
CBHW021356230426
43666CB00006B/546